# It Happened on the Lewis and Clark Expedition

## Remarkable Events That Shaped History

**Second Edition**

**Erin H. Turner**

TWODOT®

GUILFORD, CONNECTICUT
HELENA, MONTANA

# A · TWODOT® · BOOK

An imprint and registered trademark of Rowman & Littlefield

Distributed by NATIONAL BOOK NETWORK

British Library Cataloguing in Publication Information Available

**Library of Congress Cataloging-in-Publication Data**

Names: Turner, Erin H., 1973– author.
Title: It happened on the Lewis and Clark Expedition / Erin H. Turner.
Description: Helena, Montana : TwoDot, [2016] | Series: It happened in the west series | Includes bibliographical references and index.
Identifiers: LCCN 2016005454 (print) | LCCN 2016006746 (ebook) | ISBN 9781493023462 (pbk. : alk. paper) | ISBN 9781493023479 (ebook : alk. paper) | ISBN 9781493023479 (ebook)
Subjects: LCSH: Lewis and Clark Expedition (1804-1806)—Anecdotes. | West (U.S.)—Discovery and exploration—Anecdotes. | West (U.S.)—Description and travel—Anecdotes.
Classification: LCC F592.7 .T84 2016 (print) | LCC F592.7 (ebook) | DDC 917.804/2—dc23

♾™ The paper used in this publication meets the minimum requirements of American National Standard for Information Sciences—Permanence of Paper for Printed Library Materials, ANSI/NISO Z39.48-1992.

# CONTENTS

# CONTENTS

# CONTENTS

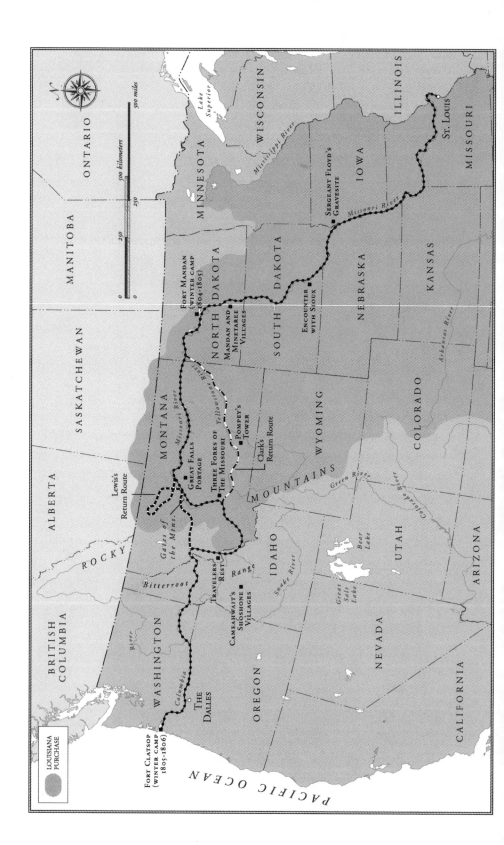

# INTRODUCTION

In 1806 there were seventeen states in the new United States of America, independence from Great Britain having been declared a mere thirty years earlier and achieved at the end of the Revolutionary War in 1781. The Constitution making the states a united whole wasn't even twenty years old. Most people who lived in the United States had never seen a map of it—let alone a map of their own state—and most certainly hadn't traveled far from home. Not only were people less mobile, the only time information moved faster than a man on horseback was on a sailboat in a strong wind. Yet, Meriwether Lewis, William Clark, and about thirty other men, one woman, and a baby, had just returned from a cross-country journey to the Pacific Ocean, cut off entirely from support from the east for most of that time. It was a marvelous feat that directed the course of US history.

It's difficult to summarize the achievements of the Corps of Discovery, as the expedition was christened, from 1804 to 1806 as they made their way across the vast territory of the Louisiana Purchase. Lists of plant and animal species identified (Lewis recorded 178 new plant species, previously unknown to science), causes advanced, and miles traveled and mapped tell part of the story. A quick overview of their journey in this day of interstate highways and sport utility vehicles tells another part. But it remains difficult to imagine the hardships and effort involved in the westward march of the small band of explorers, and even when reading their own descriptions of the journey, our modern perspective makes it difficult to comprehend.

The Corps of Discovery's epic journey was—technologically and in terms of magnitude—equal to the achievement of Neil Armstrong walking on the moon in 1969. And it took the corps more than two years with no Mission Control to rely on for support. It's no wonder the citizens of La Charrette, a small settlement on the banks of the Missouri River, were astonished to see them when their boats pulled in sight in the fall of 1806, after having left there in the spring of 1804. Everyone in La Charrette who knew about their mission had long since assumed them dead in the great unknown.

Only one man died on their expedition—an unpreventable death, most likely of appendicitis. A newborn infant joined them at a fort in what is now North Dakota in the dead of winter and traveled with his teenage mother as they crossed the country. They relied on the land to supply their food and carried their beds, shelter, and transportation with them more than eight thousand miles.

Thomas Jefferson, then president of the United States, mandated their journey, in part, with these words: "The object of your mission is to explore the Missouri River and such principal stream of it as, by its course and communication with the waters of the Pacific Ocean, may offer the most direct and practicable water communication across the continent, for the purpose of commerce."

Jefferson had just brokered the purchase of the Louisiana Territory from France's emperor, Napoleon, more than doubling the land size of the United States, and stretching its potential from "sea to shining sea." Part of his goal was to find out what species, land features, and waterways the vast wilderness held; Jefferson, a man of the Age of Enlightenment, had an avid interest in all things new. Another part was to establish trade routes to the Pacific Northwest to keep the British from forming a monopoly on the fur trade there. And another was to establish relations with the Native Americans who inhabited the vast territory. He sent his chosen representative, his secretary, Meriwether Lewis, with copious instructions and extensive preparatory training.

Lewis, a fellow Virginian, had all of the qualities that Jefferson wanted in an expedition leader. He was young, he was a skilled outdoorsman and hunter, and he had knowledge of biology, geology, and astronomy that satisfied Jefferson's ideals. Lewis, in turn, chose his dear friend William Clark to be his companion in leadership, and the two men put together a fine team of explorers for their journey. Luck certainly stepped in from time to time—Sacagawea's presence among the group helped them in many ways that they would grow to appreciate over the long miles of the trip—but skill in many things saw them through.

One of the most remarkable achievements of the expedition were the journals in which Lewis and Clark and some of the enlisted men recorded their progress across the country. No ballpoint pens accompanied them; they had to mix their ink and sharpen their quills to record the day's events in heavy leather-bound ledgers. The excerpts from those journals that appear in this book are reprinted exactly as they are found in the original. The nonstandardized spelling, punctuation, and grammar of the early nineteenth century add to the charm of these wonderful documents. Curious spelling notwithstanding, these records are among the great epics in American literature. This book contains forty-six stories of those hardships, skills, and bits of luck that made up the success of the Corps of Discovery, still fascinating more than two hundred years later.

# THE LAND DEAL OF THE CENTURY

## March 9, 1804

As the red, white, and blue banner of France rose up the flagpole over the government buildings in St. Louis, the capital of Louisiana Territory, a cheer went up from the crowd. Louisiana had been under Spanish control, and the mostly French residents of St. Louis were overjoyed at the sign of their flag waving proudly in the March breeze. The flag would only wave for a few hours, however, and then a vast expanse of land stretching west of the Missouri River would be part of the United States of America.

Captains Meriwether Lewis and William Clark were present at this transfer of power for a very good reason: When the Louisiana Territory became a United States territory, their voyage would begin. For Lewis the sight of the French tricolor rising in the air must have invited a sigh of relief—and then perhaps induced a bit of impatience, as well. He'd been preparing for this moment for more than three years. And the moment was nearly upon him.

The Louisiana Purchase, the deal necessary to make the Lewis and Clark Expedition and the westward expansion of the newly minted

United States possible, was a convoluted arrangement of signatures on paper and treaties negotiated between two great European powers and a fledgling country that had just won its independence from a third. Spain and France had been fighting for many years over land holdings in North America, and under Napoleon, France was fighting with all of Europe, as well. That fact was about to become vital to President Thomas Jefferson's plans.

As early as 1800, it was a foregone conclusion to most European powers that the United States would cross the Mississippi as its burgeoning size dictated, settling the West and claiming the land as its own Manifest Destiny. Many people at the time believed that the United States and its new government were destined to fill the North American continent.

Thomas Jefferson took an important step in the history of that transaction when he offered the job of personal secretary to a young man named Meriwether Lewis of Virginia. Under Jefferson's tutelage Lewis gained experience in cartography, natural history, medicine, and diplomacy, as well as developing other skills.

In January 1803 Jefferson sent a secret message to Congress asking for the purchase of the Louisiana Territory from France—who would first have to have it ceded to them by Spain. By making the deal, Jefferson would double the land size of the United States and develop the potential for trade in the Pacific Northwest. But to achieve that goal, Jefferson needed a survey of the territory, so he included his young secretary in his confidence long before Congress was even aware of the planned purchase.

When Jefferson approached Congress, he requested funding for a large expedition to the West to explore the new territory and to see if there was a water-based route to the Pacific. Such a route would increase the United States's trading power exponentially by cutting the three-year trip around the tip of South America to the

Pacific in half or less. And the expedition would be led by Captain Meriwether Lewis.

Lewis stood watching the flag of France rise in the air that day in St. Louis, the weighty responsibility put on him by Jefferson filling his mind. He was not yet thirty years old, and he was in charge of this massive expedition to the West Coast. His Corps of Discovery, as Jefferson called the expedition, would be the first group of Americans to visit their new land—and they had little idea what they might find.

When the largely French crowd asked that their flag fly over the city overnight, after the transfer from Spain, permission was granted. But the next day, the papers were signed, and the Stars and Stripes was raised to the sound of gunfire and shouts from the American soldiers present. Louisiana Territory was now a part of the United States.

Lewis spent a few more days in St. Louis before leaving to meet the men of the Corps of Discovery on the Missouri River, at St. Charles, finalizing plans and arrangements for supplies. As he walked its streets for the last time, he couldn't know that it would be more than three more years before he would set foot there again. It was time for the expedition to begin.

# THE FIRST DAYS ON THE RIVER

## May 14–18, 1804

A small crowd had gathered on the shore of the Missouri River that rainy May afternoon, and Sergeant John Ordway recorded the event in his journal:

> *Monday May the 14th 1804. Showery day. Capt Clark*
> *Set out at 3 oClock P.M. for the western expedition.*
> *one Gun fired. a nomber of Citizens see us Start. The*
> *party consisted of 3 Sergeants & 38 Good hands . . . we*
> *Sailed up the Missouri 6 miles & encamped.*

Finally, after the long winter of preparation, the Lewis and Clark Expedition was on the river. Two pirogues and a keelboat were loaded with supplies and trade goods; Captain Clark was in command, and Captain Lewis would be joining them in a few days up the river at St. Charles after finishing some business in St. Louis. This was their first chance to see how the boats would handle on the river, loaded with equipment. And Clark was anxious to get underway.

The keelboat was fifty-five feet long and eight feet wide. Twenty-two oars could paddle it, a sail could carry it along, or, when the river was shallow, it could be "poled" upstream as the men walked their long wooden poles from one end of the deck to the other while pushing against the bottom of the river. The boat had to be perfectly balanced, its chests and barrels arranged precisely for floating, and when it didn't float in the rocky, shallow river, they'd pull it along with ropes from the shore.

The two pirogues—shallow, open boats, one red, one white—were also loaded to the brim with supplies and with men at the oars to propel them through the water. For two days the boats slogged up the shallow Missouri, struggling upstream. But each night there was the hospitality of shore to look forward to. It was a pleasant beginning to the long-anticipated journey.

At St. Charles, the last large settlement along the Missouri River, a ball was held in the expedition's honor—and three men were court-martialed, having celebrated a bit too much and neglected their duties. It was time to leave civilization behind and start on the serious business of the cross-country trip.

For several more days they would be traveling through areas settled by whites, but Clark considered their departure from the mouth of the River Dubois on May 14, the start of the expedition.

# LEAVING LA CHARRETTE

## May 25, 1804

For nearly ten days the party of men had been moving up the swiftly flowing Missouri River in the pirogues and keelboat or walking along its shore. Settlements were increasingly rare, and their sense of departure into the vast western territory was nearly complete. The land they were entering was newly a part of the United States, and the French settlers of the Louisiana Territory greeted them with hospitality and information.

On May 24 the boats hit fast water at the "Deavels race ground," as Clark called it in his journal. As the men tried to steer the vessels and their cargo through the sharp rocks, the keelboat nearly overturned in the current. It was an ominous sign of hardships to come—and there must have been mixed emotions as the small band pulled into camp just outside of the tiny settlement of La Charrette, a village of seven families.

All along the river were settlements of mostly French traders and trappers who had moved northward for convenient hunting and trading with the local Native Americans. People from the settlements gathered on the banks to wave and shout good wishes to the explorers as they proceeded on. In La Charrette, though the village was tiny and poor, the citizens shared milk and eggs with the expedition members—the last of these staples they would see until returning to the spot more than two years hence.

But what was most important in the village of La Charrette was the information provided them by Regis Loisel, who had already been as far up the Missouri as the Mandan Indian villages in what is now North Dakota. The expedition needed the help of the Mandans and the cooperation of all of the tribes along the Missouri River. They were also mandated to establish peaceful trade with those tribes as part of their expedition. Not only had Loisel, a trader from St. Louis, explored northward along the Missouri but also south along the Arkansas River in his search for better trade with the tribes who lived there. And he'd already had a few tangles with the Sioux—one of the first tribes Lewis and Clark would encounter as they headed north.

Although neither Lewis nor Clark mentions it in their journals, and it's not known whether they were aware of the fact, they were now pushing farther north and west than one of the greatest and best-known mountain men of the time. Seventy-year-old Daniel Boone, who had settled near La Charrette and was probably aware of the expedition, may have witnessed the spectacle of the forty men, keelboat, and pirogues heading up the Missouri and into history.

# CAROLINA PARAKEETS

## June 25, 1804

The journals of the captains were effusive. The country was beautiful, wildlife abundant, and the catfish they pulled out of the river for supper were tasty and amazingly large. Even the mosquitoes and gnats, though troublesome, were a wonder to behold—their numbers and the discomfort they inflicted were not to be believed.

Nearly every day, the captains could report on the number of deer seen (and killed) and an unusual animal or bird that was in abundance as they traveled north of St. Louis, west of the Mississippi River, along the mighty Missouri. They were heading into a strange, unknown, mostly untrammeled land. Even the Native Americans they expected to see had scarcely left footprints on the earth they traveled. Every day, Clark wrote of his expectation that he'd see them in their villages. But because he didn't, he wrote about wildlife, instead. On June 25, he reported:

> *a fair morning Several hunters out to day, at 2 oClock Drewyer & Peter returned from the Otteau village, and*

*informs that no Indians were at their towns, they saw*
*Some fresh Signs of a Small party But Could not find*
*them. two Deer killed to day 1 Turkey Several Grous*
*Seen to day.*

But the most notable wildlife they saw as they passed the Blue River was a flock of small green birds. Clark reported, "I observed a great number of Parrot queets this evening."

The parakeets were probably Carolina parakeets, and this was the first time they had been mentioned as being found west of the Mississippi River. The notation was a part of the detailed account Lewis and Clark gave of 178 new plants and 122 animals—new to their eastern countrymen, not new to North America—in partial fulfillment of Thomas Jefferson's mandate to the expedition to bring back scientific information. Among the "new" birds they observed were California condors, whistling swans (as Lewis called them), and magpies. They also sent back skins, hides, and plant specimens for Jefferson's elucidation, and a live prairie dog for his entertainment.

In some cases the record written by Lewis and Clark is almost all there is left of the species. Subsequent generations have not merely left footprints on the face of the West. Instead the effects of settlement have been obvious and costly. The "parrot queet" species Clark identified that day by the Blue River is now extinct. The last green-and-yellow Carolina parakeet died in 1918, at the Cincinnati Zoo.

# THE LAST OF THE BUTTER

## July 19, 1804

Every inch of William Clark was Southern Gentleman. He traveled with his personal slave, York; he spoke and wrote with the ease of an educated mind; he rode and shot a gun admirably; and he had advanced epicurean tastes. For his thirty-fourth birthday, celebrated on the Missouri River, he ordered a feast: "a saddle of fat Vennison, an Elk fleece & a Bevertail to be cooked, and a Desert of Cheries, Plumbs, Raspberries Currents and grapes of Supr quality."

The land surrounding the Missouri River was a land of plenty. Game abounded on shore, and the hunting parties that went out in search of the meat the men required to sustain their labors didn't come back empty-handed. Already, the expedition had learned that the meat of the elk was a fine addition to their diet of venison, which they were accustomed to in their eastern homes, and the tail of the sleek, fat beavers that swam the rivers was a coveted delicacy.

On the river near what is now Council Bluffs, Iowa, and Omaha, Nebraska, the fruit of the summer was fully ripe along shore among the tall prairie grasses. The men were delighted to find plants of their acquaintance and new species—all delicious.

York probably prepared Clark's birthday supper, taking on the duties required of a manservant. It was indeed a luxurious birthday feast, one that the men would look back on with longing in the days of hunger to come. But they had to prepare it without butter or cream or eggs. The settlements of the lower Missouri were long behind them, and you can almost hear the sigh in Clark's statement of July 19, 1804, as they paused on an island for their daily rest and repast: "I call this Island Butter Island, as at this place we mad use of the last of our butter."

It would be more than two years until the Gentleman from Kentucky savored that delicacy again. For the rest of the journey, it would be game, whatever roots they could forage for, and fish . . . and sometimes horse and dog meat or nothing at all.

# THE OTTEAU VILLAGE

## July 25-August 5, 1804

"A fair morning," Captain William Clark wrote of August 1, 1804, recording yet another day of observation and delight in their new adventure. It had been a series of fair mornings for the expedition. They were easily making their way through the prairie landscape on the Platte River, sending hunters and trappers for game and tasting beaver. It was windy, and the boat rolled about so much in the water that Clark complained that he could get no work done and had to retreat to the woods to "combat with the Musquetors" to get the stillness he needed to draft his maps.

On the 27th, Clark walked ashore with Reubin Field in order to take a closer look at mounds seemingly constructed of sand and dirt next to the river and that Clark said covered about two hundred acres of land. Clark concluded that it was a former village of the "Otteaus," after spending the day exploring and returning to the boat after nightfall.

In late July, the expedition was still in territory where they expected to make contact with numerous Native American tribes that had been trading with white settlers along routes that were well established and increasingly traveled. When on the 28th of July, the sentries reported that they had heard guns to the southwest, and then George Drouillard brought in a lone Missouri whom he met while trapping on the prairie, Clark determined to meet the "Otteau."

The Oto (Clark's more fanciful spelling aside) were a very small tribe, generally made up of no more than one village. Disease and hardship had ravaged the band since the arrival of white explorers, settlers, and trappers in the area, and to all intents and purposes, the Missouri and the Oto had become one. The Missouri man who Drouillard brought into camp reported that the band was out hunting buffalo on the plains.

The captains sent a messenger to seek out the Oto to parley with them as they continued along their journey. After sending their request, they enjoyed several more days on the river, fishing and hunting, and observing the signs of a terrible storm that had ravaged the shore. They reported on Joseph Field's trapping of a badger—Clark describing the unfamiliar character in exuberant detail—and enjoyed the wild raspberries, grapes, and other fruits that grew along the shore. And when they sent two men out to recover two horses that went missing, they instructed one of them to return to the spot from which the messenger to the Oto had set out. Clark wrote, "The Indians not yet arrived we fear Something amiss with our messenger or them."

Clark's words and descriptions from those days, even those about boils and "tumers" afflicting the men, ring with enthusiasm even after two centuries. But the hesitation and worry reflects the gravity of the expedition's undertaking. The next day, when the Oto and the horses made their way into camp, it was surely a relief and a sign to the captains of the promise of the exploration to come.

# DESERTION

## August 18, 1804

The Corps of Discovery had been encamped for nearly a week, and the week had been a mix of success and failure. The eighteenth of August was an auspicious occasion, the thirtieth birthday of Captain Meriwether Lewis—and a fine evening ended with a dance that lasted until eleven o'clock. The group had been visited that day by the chiefs of the Otos and Missouris, an object of their camp. And Private Reed, a man missing from the expedition for ten days, had returned to camp.

The expedition had been hoping for days to meet up with the Omaha, Oto, and Missouri Indians, hoping to broker a peace between the warring tribes on the Missouri and open up trade possibilities to the north of St. Louis. The Omahas were on a bison hunt and never met with the expedition, but the Otos and Missouris arrived with the hope that Lewis and Clark would help them make peace with their neighbors. But in spite of some success in their negotiations and the birthday celebration, not all was well in the Corps of Discovery.

Private Moses B. Reed was desperately unhappy. The minimal privations of their first summer on the river had proved too much for the young man, and at Council Bluffs he had announced that he had left his knife behind and was going back for it. The knives were of utmost importance to the expedition—as Clark had impressed upon them when they were given out before the start of the voyage—and to leave it would have meant hardship for everyone. But days went by after he left to retrieve it, and Reed did not return.

Another man, a French civilian working for the expedition, was also missing. And it was strongly suspected that both had deserted. The captains sent a small party of four men to bring them back, and they gave the order to shoot Reed if he did not surrender peaceably. Discipline was even more important than a sharp knife blade. The officers had to maintain a strict control over the men in their charge in order to assure the success of their mission. And desertion was a military crime punishable by death.

On August 18 Private Reed arrived in camp accompanied by the search party. The Frenchman had not been found. Reed confessed that desertion was his plan—and he also confessed to the charge of stealing Army property, his gun and ammunition.

The captains responded with their punishment: Reed would not be put to death, but he would not go without a severe penalty for his actions. The party formed two lines and beat him with switches as he ran the gauntlet four times, passing between them to receive his punishment. This was a shrewd move by the two captains; it didn't devastate morale, but it did demonstrate their will and concern for discipline.

However somber the mood after Reed's punishment, the day ended gaily with the celebration of Lewis's thirtieth birthday. The Frenchman was never found, but Reed was allowed to winter with the men at Fort Mandan. In the spring he returned to St. Louis with a party dispatched from the fort to take specimens and letters east to Jefferson. He had lost his place in history as a member of the permanent expedition, but he will always be remembered as its one deserter.

# A FALLEN COMRADE

## August 20, 1804

The night of August 18, 1804, was one of celebration for the men who had come up the Missouri River with Lewis and Clark. It was Lewis's thirtieth birthday, and each had an extra dram of whiskey and danced until eleven o'clock at night, accompanied by the sweet sounds of Pierre Cruzatte's fiddle. But Sergeant Charles Floyd was not in the best of spirits. He had been ill for some time.

Charles Floyd was only twenty-one or twenty-two years old and perfectly fit the characteristics Lewis and Clark had looked for in the men chosen to accompany them to the Pacific. He was one of three sergeants and was well liked by the men in his command and his commanders. Captain Clark and Sergeant Ordway both commented on his illness as early as July 30. On July 31 Ordway wrote, "Sergeant Floyd has been Sick Several days but now is Gitting some better."

Lewis was the "doctor" in the bunch, having learned herbal remedies at his mother's knee and studied with the famous Dr. Benjamin Rush in Philadelphia before setting out on the journey. But even his training wouldn't have been enough. In fact it might have made Sergeant Floyd even worse.

In 1804 doctors knew very little about what caused illness. Most believed that the body was made up of four humors—one of which was blood—and that illnesses were caused by having too much of one humor or not enough of the others. Lewis treated Floyd as best he knew how, by bleeding him to rid him of his excess "bad blood" and giving him a purgative to make him empty his stomach because that was where the trouble seemed to lie.

After a long night of watching, on the morning of August 20, 1804, the party set out upriver. Clark had stayed up all night the previous night with the sick man and wrote in his journal that Floyd was as sick "as he can be to live." His words would be prophetic. The next day, when the expedition stopped to make Floyd a warm bath to try to make him more comfortable, he died, saying to Clark, "I am going away . . . I want you to write me a letter."

The expedition buried Floyd on a bluff near today's Sioux City, Iowa. They named the bluff and the nearby river that fed the Missouri after him.

Floyd was the only member of the expedition to die during their epic cross-country journey. His comrades remembered him in their writings as they crossed the country and when they paused at his bluff and river the following spring.

On August 22, 1804, the expedition made history by holding the first election by Americans west of the Mississippi. The men elected Patrick Gass their new sergeant. Interestingly, Gass was the longest-lived member of the expedition. He lived until 1870—he was nearly one hundred years old.

# REUNION

## September 11, 1804

The captains had begun to give up hope. Surely, young George Shannon had not been able to survive so long on his own in this unfamiliar, hostile territory. Surely, he wouldn't be able to find his way back to them in this vast wilderness. Now that John Colter had searched and returned to the party without finding him, it appeared that the expedition might have lost another member, following the death of Sergeant Floyd less than a month earlier. What did this foretell for the rest of their journey?

On August 26 Shannon had gone out to hunt for the expedition's horses with George Drouillard, under orders to keep to the high lands and follow the rest of the party along the river. The next day, Drouillard returned without the horses or Shannon.

Privates Joseph Field and John Shields were next on the Shannon search detail, but they walked all night and found no sign of him. Where could Shannon be? And was he well? Could he possibly have eaten in the past three days? These questions must have plagued his commanding officers as they walked along.

Finally, at a camp called Calumet Bluff, they spotted tracks—Shannon was ahead of them. He must have rushed to catch up and passed them instead. John Colter set off looking for him again, and for several days the expedition followed Colter's tracks, which were in turn following Shannon's tracks up the river. But when Colter returned, on September 6, he still had not found George Shannon.

Five days later, the mood was somber. What had happened to the young man? Was it possible that he was still up ahead of them? How could he be alive after sixteen days with no support and nothing to eat?

The keelboat pushed forward up the Missouri River on September 11, keeping to its arduous upriver path. And there was Shannon—standing calmly on shore, waiting for a trading boat. He had grown sure that he'd never catch up with the expedition, not knowing all along that they were behind him.

Shannon had survived extremely well in the wilderness on his own, eating wild grapes and one rabbit, "which he Killed by shooting a piece of hard stick" after he ran out of ammunition. It's easy to imagine the ribbing the young man must have gotten for his lack of meat in a land full of game—and for leading the expedition upriver the whole time he thought he was following them.

Shannon survived the expedition, though he was separated from the group more than once after that, but never for so long. He was one of the better-educated enlisted men along for the journey, and he later helped Nicholas Biddle edit the first published edition of the journals and served as a US senator from Missouri. Perhaps managing to kill a rabbit with a stick when you're hungry is more impressive than killing an antelope with a gun.

# ENCOUNTER WITH THE SIOUX

## September 25–28, 1804

A group had gathered along the river to hear what the white men had to say and to take their presents. Meriwether Lewis stood beneath the flag on shore and began painstakingly conveying his message to the Sioux.

The poor translation of Lewis's words heard by the Sioux as they gathered in a band under the flags near shore didn't help; they showed no interest in words, only in the trade goods the expedition had with them. So, after sharing a ceremonial pipe, the captains invited three "chiefs," Black Buffalo, Partisan, and Buffalo Medicine, on board the magnificent keelboat in the river.

All during their journey, Lewis and Clark had heard about the mysterious and feared Sioux Indians whom they would encounter on their way into the Mandan territories. The Sioux had a fierce reputation among the French and Spanish traders who had previously made their way into this territory.

But on September 25, 1804, when they had their first encounter, the young braves strung their bows, an action that usually inspired fear in the white traders who made it this far up the river. There were two camps with about 140 lodges, near what is today Pierre, South Dakota, and such a large group could easily have overcome the small band of explorers. Undaunted, the captains stood their ground, and because they showed no fear, the Sioux did not attack—perhaps purely out of curiosity about this strange band, who were not traders or merchants and merely wanted to move up the river.

Black Buffalo, once on the keelboat, wasn't going to let them off easy, though. After the corps shared whiskey with the Sioux chiefs, the three became belligerent, and Partisan feigned drunkenness, as Clark said, so that he could hide his true intentions. Clark quickly got them off the boat and into the pirogue, but as they reached the shore, three young men seized the pirogue's rope, and there was a scuffle on the boat as Partisan stumbled against Clark. Partisan demanded additional presents and behaved in such a threatening manner that Clark drew his sword, and from on board the keelboat, Lewis called his men to arms.

Black Buffalo ordered the young men with the rope away, but Clark was brought on shore, and the braves with their strung bows pulled their arrows from their quivers. The other men in the pirogue returned to the keelboat to bring back to shore a larger armed group. When the pirogue returned, apparently the Sioux thought better of their actions and allowed Clark to head off to the boat and rejoin his men, but relations with the chiefs had been strained. They would not shake Clark's hand when offered on shore.

Clark did not sleep all that night, and the next day when the chiefs asked that the expedition stay another night, Lewis went ashore with a small group. The chiefs said they just wanted the women and children to see the boats, but after Lewis had been gone three hours, Clark became suspicious and sent a sergeant to seek his friend. No harm had come to Lewis. He reported back that there was to be a grand feast that night—and the expedition was treated to a feast of delicacies, such as buffalo hump, dog, and prairie potato, a turnip-like root.

After the feast the captains returned to their boat, intending to move upriver, but again they were stayed by Indians seeking tobacco and Chief Partisan declaring that they had to pay more in trade goods before they'd be allowed to go. Eventually, on September 28 they were able to pull away from the shores teeming with two hundred armed Sioux and travel on up the dangerous river.

# CRUZATTE AND THE GREAT WHITE BEAR

October 20, 1804

Almost from the moment the Corps of Discovery first pulled their keelboat and pirogues onto the Missouri River, the legend of the Great White Bear began to grow. Trappers who worked the Missouri River warned them of a ferocious beast that was larger and more lethal than any of the black bears of the East. Native Americans that they met along the river wore necklaces of bear claws—each three times longer than those belonging to their ursine relatives familiar to the expedition. And on October 20, 1804, Captain William Clark recorded in his journal, "I saw Several fresh track of those animals which is 3 times as large as a mans track."

But Clark's encounter with a track was not the only grizzly encounter that day. Pierre Cruzatte came back to camp with a tale that defied all previous American experience with bears.

In some ways it was surprising that Pierre Cruzatte stepped into grizzly bear history that day—and in some ways it was not. Cruzatte was blind in one eye and nearsighted in the other, a fact that

Meriwether Lewis would become painfully aware of on their return trip to the East when a gun-wielding Cruzatte mistook him for an elk. Even so, St. Peter, as the men on the trip called him, was a superb hunter, fluent in the Omaha language, skilled in sign language, and an ace fiddle player who entertained the men with style on their long journey.

Because of his skill as a hunter, Cruzatte was often among the parties that went into the plains in pursuit of the expedition's daily ration of meat. He brought in elk, venison, and bison—the large ungulates of the prairie—on a regular basis. By October 20 the party was well into what is now North Dakota, where no grizzly now resides, but which was then part of the wide range of this massive carnivore. Clark may have seen a footprint, but Cruzatte was about to see the real thing.

Lewis recorded the event in his journal: "Peter Crusat this day shot at a white bear he wounded him, but being alarmed at the formidable appearance of the bear he left his tomahalk and gun; but shortly after returned and found that the bear had taken the oposite rout."

The fearless Cruzatte, hunter of big game, had met his match in the giant bear. In the vast prairie of North Dakota, the animal must have loomed large, indeed, over the small, wiry man with two bad eyes. It's no wonder he turned and ran—but because the bear did the same, and in the opposite direction, he retrieved his tomahawk and gun and returned to hunt another day.

The retreat of the grizzly was a portent of change to come. A hundred years later, there were no grizzlies to be found in North Dakota or anywhere on the Great Plains. Today, they inhabit only remote areas of Montana, Wyoming, and Idaho as well as Alaska. The Corps of Discovery blazed the way for the wave of trappers, then settlers, who moved into the bear's historic range.

# LIFE AMONG THE MANDANS

## November 20, 1804

The river was frozen and the wind was icy cold as it whipped across the plains and into and around the small huts built by the Corps of Discovery. They could go no farther this winter. They had built a fort and would stay within sight of the Mandan and Hidatsa villages on the upper Missouri River.

The Mandans and Hidatsas were Great Plains tribes that had been decimated by smallpox brought north by traders on the Missouri and by war with the Sioux. They had four small villages on the west side of the Missouri River, and the captains built their fort on the east side.

The Corps of Discovery had much to do that winter: They copied out detailed notes about the tribes they'd met so far on their journey, the plants and animals they'd encountered, and their astronomical observations. Map making occupied much of their time, as did preparing specimens of bird skeletons and animal hides to send back to President Jefferson. The keelboat that had been their home and supply ship for the trip up the Missouri would be going down the river in the spring with their eastbound packages aboard. In case the expedition did not return from the Pacific, the thinking was, their efforts would not be a total loss.

The Mandans were excellent neighbors, supplying corn for winter's use, but they were skeptical of the expedition's intentions. As farmers who traded with the English, the French, and other Indians, they weren't strangers to the promises of whites who wanted to establish trade relationships with this peaceful nation. Black Cat, their chief, spent many hours in council with the expedition—he was extremely interested in the guns and ammunition for which he might trade to protect his people from the predations of other tribes on the Missouri.

Clark remarked of the Mandans, "The Mandans are at war with all who make war only, and wish to be at peace with all nations, Seldom the ogressors."

Establishing a relationship with these peaceful Mandans seemed an excellent start to the diplomatic negotiations required of the expedition, but differences in culture were difficult to ignore. With such close contact between the tribe and the white men of the expedition, conflicts were not uncommon, particularly regarding the status of the Indian women. And rumors of trade relationships and alliances between tribes caused upset more than once. But the captains thought that the most important object of the expedition's winter with the Mandans—gathering information about the journey to come—was achieved and all trouble was handled peacefully.

After the expedition moved into its fort, called Mandan, they received visits from traders on the upper Missouri and representatives of many different tribes. Everyone who came to visit was quizzed about his knowledge of the vast expanse to the west. And the expedition was satisfied with the information.

The Mandans informed them that crossing the Rocky Mountains would take a mere half day by horseback up the east side—and the captains were well pleased. In fact it would take them more than two weeks to portage the Great Falls of the Missouri, and they would not see Fort Mandan again for nearly two years.

# "MORE COLD THAN I THOUGHT IT POSSIBLE"

## January 10, 1805

Their first Christmas in the wilderness had come and gone, as the Corps of Discovery entered their third month in the hut shelters of Fort Mandan. The ice on the Missouri was thick, allowing for visits with the Mandans on the west side of the river, and the air was cold—perhaps especially so for these young men from Kentucky and Virginia. The pleasures of the winter at the fort had been many, but the long, dark days wore on, and the cold grew steadily worse. It was January on the northern plains.

On January 9, 1805, Clark recorded in his journal: "a Cold Day Thermometer at 21° below 0, great numbers of indians go to kill Cows, the little Crow Brackft. with us, Several Indians Call at the Fort nearly frosed."

The mercury continued to drop, and Clark reported that the temperature was forty below zero when he rose on the morning of January 10.

The day before, a party of Mandan men had gone out to hunt, and a man and boy had not returned. A search party came to Fort Mandan to ask for the loan of a sleigh so that they might go looking for the lost men, out all night in the bitter cold with no fire and no protection. Clark fully expected that they would find them, but frozen to death. But the two missing Mandans made their way back to the fort. The boy, who was only thirteen, arrived in the morning with frostbitten feet that the captains treated. The man came in unharmed by his night out in the cold. Clark's journal entry continued:

> *about 10 oClock the boy about 13 years of age Came to the fort with his feet frosed and had layed out last night without fire with only a Buffalow Robe to Cover him, the Dress which he wore was a pr. of Cabra Legins, which is verry thin and mockersons we had his feet put in cold water and they are, Comeing too. Soon after the arrival of the Boy, a Man Came in who had also Stayed out without fire, and verry thinly Clothed, this man was not the least injured. Customs &: the habits of those people has anured to bare more Cold than I thought it possible for man to endure.*

Staying out in that weather was an astonishing feat. And it undoubtedly taught the captains about the effects of the severe cold. It was possible that they would have another winter's encampment ahead of them when they reached the west side of the Rocky Mountains the following fall. Crossing the plains or the mountains in winter was foolhardy, and they planned to get an early start on the remainder of their journey once the temperatures warmed.

## A BABY JOINS THE EXPEDITION

# February 11, 1805

Sacagawea was miserable. She was all alone in the fort built by the whites at her adopted Mandan village—the only woman, and hardly a woman. She was probably thirteen or fourteen years old. For hours she had been in labor. The pains were agonizing, and she was exhausted. Otter Woman, another wife of Toussaint Charbonneau, was not allowed in the fort to come care for her. Otter Woman had been left behind when the young, pregnant Sacagawea and her husband had joined the Lewis and Clark Expedition.

Sacagawea was not a Mandan or Minetaree Indian. She was a Shoshone—the "Snake Indians," as they were called by many whites. Several years before, when she was about eleven years old, her people had been attacked by the Minetarees, or "Big Bellies," as they were encamped by the Three Forks of the Missouri River in present-day Montana. The Minetarees had killed most of the Shoshone band, but the young girls were taken as slaves.

In some ways the life that Sacagawea led with the Minetarees was better than her life with the Shoshone. She learned the language, and she learned the ways of a farming people (the Shoshone had been nomadic, dependent on the movements of the herds for food). The Minetaree almost always had plenty to eat. That was why they were called the Big Bellies. She was adopted by the women of the tribe and given a woman's belt of blue beads—a mark of honor. The women of the Minetaree hoped that she would marry into the tribe.

It's not clear why the young woman instead became the wife of Toussaint Charbonneau, a part-French trapper who made his home with the Minetaree. Charbonneau already had a wife, Otter Woman, and a son, and was much older than Sacagawea. Otter Woman was also a Shoshone—but from a different band. Sacagawea must have wanted to speak her native language with her new family, but Charbonneau would not allow it. They were only to speak the Minetaree or Hidatsa (or Mandan) language and the few words of French he taught them.

During the winter of 1804 and 1805, Toussaint Charbonneau and his wives were living at the Mandan villages on the Missouri River. Sacagawea must have been surprised when the band of white men rowed their big boats up the river and made camp. They built houses and a wall around them—a log fort to keep them safe. Everything about the strange men was fascinating. They had a big black dog with them that didn't do any work—and a black man named York traveled with them. Charbonneau told his wives that York was William Clark's slave. But the Minetaree were fascinated by him and thought his black skin was somehow magical.

Charbonneau made friends with the whites, and he was hired to join them as their guide when they went west. Sacagawea was already far along in her pregnancy when Charbonneau shared this news with the two women. She must have been alarmed when next he told her that she was coming along on the expedition, that she would speak to her people in Shoshone and tell him the words in Hidatsa, then he would tell them in French to a translator who would turn them into English for Captains Lewis and Clark.

On the night that she was in labor, she could barely communicate with those around her. She was young, and she was frightened. The pains grew worse—and still the baby did not come.

Eventually, Lewis came to see her himself. He had brought a good deal of medical equipment with him for the expedition, but no one had thought to provide for the possible birth of a baby on the way. After all, the expedition was made up only of men! He looked through his kit, but there was nothing to help the poor, suffering girl.

Then, a trader, Jussome, who lived in the Mandan village, had an idea. He had heard that crushing the rattle of a rattlesnake and taking the powder would make the baby come.

Lewis broke up bits of rattle and gave it to Sacagawea in water. And very soon after, the small boy was born.

Charbonneau named the little child Jean Baptiste, after his father. But Sacagawea called him Pomp, which means "first born" in the Shoshone language. And that's what the expedition members called him as he traveled first in the cradleboard and then as a toddler with the expedition as they crossed to the Pacific Ocean and returned to the Mandan villages. He was now the youngest member of the expedition, and Sacagawea, his mother, was the next youngest.

## CHARBONNEAU DECLARES HE WON'T GO

## March 12, 1805

The wind was fierce and the cold of March was still in the air as the little family packed its belongings and moved out of Fort Mandan. Tiny Jean Baptiste, barely a month old, was surely bundled against the cold as they made their way back to the lodges of the Mandan on the other side of the river. Charbonneau had declared his intentions: He would not go west with the expedition, and neither would his family.

The territory that Lewis and Clark and their men set out to investigate had been in American hands for only a few months, and in the years and decades before that, it had passed back and forth between the Spanish and French—and all of this was mostly unknown to the indigenous peoples who for centuries had lived there, hunted there, and died there. As French trappers and traders had made their way up and down the Missouri River, some of those indigenous peoples had come in contact with them, gained technology and goods from them, and picked up bits of their language, too.

And some of the French trappers and traders had learned the native languages, as well. But almost no one on the upper Missouri outside of Lewis and Clark's small band spoke English. It was essential to the expedition that they hire translators to come along with them to help them communicate with the tribes along their route. They needed supplies and they needed information—and there was nowhere else to get it for almost two thousand miles.

At first glance Pierre Toussaint Charbonneau looked like an unlikely prospect for the journey. He had been living with the Mandans and other upper Missouri Indians for years, and true, he spoke French and Hidatsa. But he also had several wives and children, including the infant that Lewis had helped deliver that cold night in February, Jean Baptiste.

As a bargainer Charbonneau was a failure. And when he began to make demands on the captains, the things the man wanted were outrageous.

Charbonneau said that unless the captains gave him their promise that he wouldn't have to work, except as an interpreter—no carrying, paddling, standing guard, or other duties—and unless they agreed that if he was dissatisfied with the expedition, he could depart with as many provisions as he chose to carry, he, Toussaint Charbonneau, would not go with them up the Missouri and neither would his young Shoshone wife, Sacagawea.

Lewis and Clark must have shrugged their shoulders and made other arrangements. Who wanted to travel with this smelly, fat Frenchman anyway? And he was bringing along his young wife and son, as well. They might be better off without them.

Clark might have wondered about the bargain they later struck when he made this notation in his journal on March 17.

*Mr. Chabonah Sent a frenchman of our party [to say]
that he was Sorry for the foolish part he had acted and
if we pleased he would accompany us agreeabley to the
terms we had perposed and doe every thing we wished
him to doe &c. &c. he had requested me Some thro our
French inturpeter two days ago to excuse his Simplicity
and take him into the cirvice, after he had taken his
things across the River we called him in and Spoke
to him on the Subject, he agreed to our tirms and we
agreed that he might go on with us &c. &c.*

So, Sacagawea must have bundled her young son, again, and carried him back into Fort Mandan for the weeks that remained until
the expedition moved on. And surely the captains wondered about
the bargain when Charbonneau nearly upset a pirogue and when the
translations called for his wife, Sacagawea, to speak to him in Hidatsa,
for him to speak to Drouillard in French, and Drouillard to speak to
the captains in English. But one thing was certain, without Charbonneau, Sacagawea would not have accompanied the men across
country—and her presence proved invaluable.

# THE ICE BREAKUP

## March 29, 1805

The smells, sights, and sounds of spring drifted in the cool breeze that refreshed Fort Mandan and its occupants. The winter had been given to preparations for the journey, the hard work of mending equipment and putting up supplies, tedious in the flickering light of lamps and candles. But every night, as warm weather and the journey's renewal approached, the men danced and frolicked with the Mandan Indians.

As Lewis and Clark grew anxious to leave, the signs of the land's rebirth were all around them. Swans and wild geese flew north overhead, returning from their winter's sojourn in the south. And the snow and ice were giving way to fresh green prairie grass and rushing water. Fewer Indians were visiting as the river between their lodges and the fort filled with the chunks of ice, signaling the breakup of the winter's footpath and the renewed navigability of the expedition's passage to the West.

A flurry of activity filled the fort as preparations for the journey commenced. The permanent party was preparing to go west as soon as the river was safe, and the detachment was getting ready to go back to the United States to report to President Thomas Jefferson. These men would travel with the spoils of the expedition thus far, including plant specimens, letters, and one prairie dog.

The captains, who had spent most of the winter gathering as much information as they could about what they might encounter in the Great Plains and Rocky Mountains, must have chafed as the days went by as they waited for the ice to melt.

While the preparations were going on at Fort Mandan, the tribe across the river was engaging in spring activities, as well. Clark noted in his journal: "I observed extrodanary dexterity of the Indians in jumping from one cake of ice to another, for the purpose of Catching the buffalow as they float down many of the cakes of ice which they pass over are not two feet square. The Plains are on fire in View of the fort on both Sides of the River."

For the Mandan the lean winter months were over—the first buffalo of the season had floated down the swollen river to provide food and more, and the hunting season was just a short time away.

The captains must have felt joy at the abundance of springtime and delight at the continuation of their journey. But in spite of all of their information-gathering over the winter, they didn't know that all of their hardship was ahead of them, or even that what would be a summer of plenty for the Mandans would be a test of their skill, mettle, and endurance as the expedition traveled on to the Pacific.

# GRIZZLY ENCOUNTERS

## April 29, 1805

Captain Lewis walked along the shore—as he often did, preferring steady ground beneath his feet to the motion of the small boats in the rushing river—recording the number of animals and beauty of the landscape around them. After a long, cold winter with the Mandans at the fort on the Missouri, the crisp breezes of spring were a delight to the men as they made their way west.

The animals were abundant, and the species diverse. Elk, bison, pronghorn, deer, wolves, and grizzly bears dotted the landscape on either side of the river. Other than Pierre Cruzatte's brief encounter with the grizzly that he wounded the previous fall, the expedition had yet to experience the great bear other than through the reports of others and the claws they'd seen hanging long and menacing on the necklaces of Native Americans they'd met on the way. Paw prints proved the size of these animals, but they had yet to kill one.

Bears were a valuable commodity—in addition to the large quantity of meat, they also produced oil from their fat, and the hides were extremely thick and durable—but the expedition must also have been interested in them as a species, and interested in vanquishing one just to see if they could do it. Grizzly bears were unknown in the East.

Lewis reported of his journey on shore on April 29.

*I walked on shore with one man. about 8. a.m. we fell in with two brown or yellow bear; both of which we wounded; one of them made his escape, the other after my firing on him pursued me seventy or eighty yards, but fortunately had been so badly wounded that he was unable to pursue me so closely as to prevent my charging my gun; we again repeated our fir and killed him. it was a male not fully grown, we estimated his weight at 300 lbs. not having the means of ascertaining it precisely. The legs of this bear are somewhat longer than those of the black, as are it's tallons and tusks incomparably larger and longer.*

It was the first grizzly kill of the expedition, a small bear that Lewis examined closely and reported on in detail, ending his account with the comment, "in the hands of skillfull riflemen they are by no means as formidable or dangerous as they have been represented."

Lewis would change his opinion. Over the next few days, they saw grizzlies everywhere. And their success in dealing with them was mixed. Six days later, Clark went out with George Drouillard, and it took ten bullets to kill a bear that was "the largest of the carnivorous kind I ever saw."

In his measurements of that bear, Lewis reported, "it was a most tremendious looking animal, and extremely hard to kill notwithstanding he had five balls through his lungs and five others in various parts he swam more than half the distance across the river to a sand-bar, & it was at least twenty minutes before he died."

The experience with the bears was impressive. A few days later, when one of the party wounded a bear on his own, he did not pursue it to the end of the battle. The bears had won the respect of even the rifle-wielding mountain men.

# SACAGAWEA SAVES THE DAY

## May 14, 1805

The fierce wind swayed the tall prairie grasses still green with the ripeness of spring. All around the wide and rapid Missouri River, there were signs of pronghorn, bison, prairie dogs, and deer. The Corps of Discovery had split up: a party on land to hunt for the men's rations; crews in the low, flat pirogues, guiding them with sails unfurled; and Captains Lewis and Clark striding ahead in the glorious sunshine.

Suddenly, a shout went up from the pirogue Toussaint Charbonneau was steering. His wife, Sacagawea, and young son, Pomp, were on board along with several other crew members. A gust of wind had rocked the heavily laden boat and waves were crashing over the sides.

Toussaint Charbonneau completely lost his head as he flailed about in the small boat, trying to keep himself dry. He could not swim, and he could not gather his resources to put his hand back on the tiller. Instead, his inexperience caused him to turn the sail so that the boat tipped onto its side! And after the sail was cut and the boat was righted, it was filled almost to the top with Missouri River water. Precious cargo floated into the river from the back of the canoe.

Charbonneau had gotten the expedition in a similar fix just a month before, when they'd nearly lost another canoe as waves rocked it in a storm. The winds on the Missouri were very high, and his inexperience at the tiller and volatile temper made him an unfit helmsman. Still, every man had to take his turn at the many jobs of the expedition: hunting, rowing, cooking, sewing, and more. Every inch they moved up the Missouri was done on foot or against the current of the great river. The sails improved the forward motion but did little for stability in the high prairie winds. And Toussaint Charbonneau did no better the second time winds buffeted his boat.

Pierre Cruzatte was also on board the little pirogue, and he leapt to the tiller as Charbonneau became increasingly hysterical. Leveling his gun at his incoherent countryman, he growled out orders to the other men and threatened to shoot Charbonneau if he didn't "do his duty." Instantly, two of the other men on board began bailing out the water that was dragging the heavy pirogue under the high waves. Two others began frantically rowing toward shore with Cruzatte.

No one thought to give Charbonneau's Shoshone wife, Sacagawea, an order, but she remained calm as well, plucking items out of the water at the back of the boat as they started to drift away.

The wet and exhausted group stopped the next day to assess the damage and dry out. A rainfall halted their progress, but when they were eventually able to take inventory, Lewis noted that although the medicines were seriously damaged and several other items were ruined, tragedy had been averted.

Lewis recalled the events in his journal, crediting Cruzatte for his quick thinking and heaping equal praise on the young woman. He wrote: "The Indian woman, to whom I ascribe equal fortitude and resolution with any person on board at the time of the accident, caught and preserved most of the light articles which were washed overboard."

The items that were floating away that day on the river included papers, instruments, books, medicine, and most of the trade goods the expedition would need to buy passage across the Rocky Mountains and were, Lewis said, "indispensibly necessary to . . . insure the success of the enterprize in which, we are now launched."

# SEAMAN AND THE BEAVER

## May 19, 1805

The Mandan Indians didn't know what to make of York, Clark's black slave—men weren't slaves, only women, and they had never seen a man of such dark skin before—and they certainly didn't know what to think of a dog who had a name and was never required to work. Their dogs pulled their travois and worked around camp. Seaman, Meriwether Lewis's Newfoundland, was part of the team and an honored pet.

The great black dog bounded along the shore of the Missouri River after his master. He had made the long journey from Virginia as a member of the expedition, and already he was proving useful, even if he wasn't "working" as the Mandans thought he should.

Once, he even captured and killed a pronghorn and brought it back to the men for butchering. He was a good hunter, and he was helpful when they encountered other animals along the trail. Bison seemed wary of him—and the pronghorn and deer were rightly so.

Seaman's curiosity got the better of him, though, with a rodent in the river.

When the Lewis and Clark Expedition went west along the Missouri River, people were already aware that the Pacific Northwest was teeming with animals that could be used for fur. England had substantial holdings in what is now Canada, and trading ships made their way to present-day Washington and Oregon regularly to meet with the members of the Hudson's Bay Company and trade for the valuable furs.

One of the most important fur animals lived in the waters of the northern forests and also along rivers in Montana, South Dakota, and North Dakota: the beaver. In a few years after the expedition, the West would be full of trappers searching for the industrious animals with the sleek dark fur whose hides brought in a tidy profit. Beaver hats were all the rage for the fashionable, and they commanded a high price. When Lewis and Clark passed through, the native inhabitants trapped beaver for food and for its pelts. Roasted beaver tail was considered a delicacy.

Seaman must have seen the sleek head move under the water and gone after it. Newfoundlands are strong swimmers, with giant paws and webbed toes. The pronghorn that Seaman caught had been in the water, too. But he didn't know that beavers have two very long, sharp teeth—their livelihood depends on them. They gnaw trees and fell them to make elaborate beaver dams and lodges.

This time, the beaver gnawed Seaman.

A giant, black, dripping-wet dog limped its way back to camp. The gash in his leg was deep, and he was bleeding heavily. Clark wrote in his journal, "Captain Lewis's dog was badly bitten by a wounded beaver and was near bleeding to death."

Lewis stopped everything when he saw his wounded dog—all of the medicines in his chest and all of his skills went to work on his beloved pet.

Seaman recovered—and he made it all the way to the Pacific Ocean and back with the men of the expedition. His participation in the expedition as the dog who went to the Pacific with Lewis and Clark is commemorated by statues all over the West.

# LEWIS SEES THE MOUNTAINS

## May 26, 1805

The Missouri River grew shallower every day, and the men strained to put their paddles into the water to shove the little pirogues along. On either bank were steep, chalky cliffs, white and yellow, and sparsely vegetated. Surely, the shining mountains and great falls that the Mandans and their visitors had discussed all winter must be approaching.

The expedition, which now included a woman and a baby in its ranks, had been moving west from the Mandan villages and their winter home for nearly a month. The big sky of the plains stretched wide over the little boats and their inhabitants. Elk were frequent sights along shore and frequent entrees at dinner. Grizzlies and bison and pronghorn and prairie dogs completed the newness of the landscape.

Over the winter with the Mandan Indians, Lewis and Clark collected information about the journey to the Pacific that was ahead of them. It was their great hope—and that of President Thomas Jefferson—that they would find an all-water passage to the Pacific through the northern part of the Louisiana Purchase land. At that time the only thing that moved faster than a horse and rider was a boat under sail, backed by a stiff wind and a strong current. An all-water route to the Pacific Ocean would open up trade and other opportunities to the new United States.

But, as the days passed during the winter, Lewis and Clark could find no one who knew of an all-water route. And as they crossed what is now Montana, finding one must have seemed less and less likely.

From their information they knew that before reaching the Rocky Mountains, there would be a series of great waterfalls on the Missouri for the expedition to navigate with their canoes, equipment, and supplies. And then they knew that the mountains would rise up and have to be crossed—probably by horse. They thought that the portage around the Great Falls would take a day, or perhaps two. Their information told them that they could ascend the front of the Rocky Mountains in a day's ride. Having been away from home for a year already, Lewis, Clark, and their men must have looked forward every day to the appearance of those mountains and the "beginning of the end" that they represented. Perhaps, they'd even be home by Christmas!

Lewis spent much of his time out of the canoes, walking along shore—making notes for his journal about the landscape, the wildlife, and their position. On the afternoon of May 26, he climbed the steep cliffs on either side of the shallow, difficult river and later wrote in his journal:

> *In the after part of the day I also walked out and ascended the river hills which I found sufficiently fortiegueing. on arriving to the summit [of] one of the highest points in the neighbourhood I thought myself well repaid for my labour; as from this point I beheld the Rocky Mountains for the first time, I could only discover a few of the most elivated points above the*

*horizon, the most remarkable of which by my pocket*
*compass I found bore N. 65° W. being a little to the N.*
*of the N.W. extremity of the range of broken mountains*
*seen this morning by Capt. C. these points of the Rocky*
*Mountains were covered with snow and the sun shone*
*on it in such manner as to give me the most plain and*
*satisfactory view. while I viewed these mountains I*
*felt a secret pleasure in myself so near the head of the*
*heretofore conceived boundless Missouri; but when I*
*reflected on the difficulties which this snowey barrier*
*would most probably throw in my way to the Pacific,*
*and the sufferings and hardships of myself and party in*
*thim, it in some measure counterballanced the joy I had*
*felt in the first moments in which I gazed on them; but*
*as I have always held it a crime to anticipate evils I will*
*believe it a good comfortable road untill I am compelled*
*to believe differently.*

In a few days Lewis and his crew would come to believe differently, but for the moment they were in sight of the end of the Missouri River and the beginning of the shining mountains.

# THE MISSOURI OR THE MARIAS

## June 4-10, 1805

More than a week had passed since the expedition had spotted the Rocky Mountains in the distance, and the weather had been awful. Rain, snow, and wind buffeted them as they passed through land that became increasingly flat even with the peaks in the distance—but also increasingly wooded and full of game. The hunters were busy supplying food and elk hides for the journey's needs, and everyone watched as wolves, bison, pronghorn, and elk moved about the land. But in front of them was a question: Which river should they take?

The Missouri, which vacillated between narrow and shallow and wide and raging as it passed through the northern plains, had come to a fork. One tine stretched north and west, the other south and west—and with no map to guide them and no information save that of the men they'd questioned all winter long, there was no obvious answer.

Lewis and Clark believed, from all of their information gathering over the winter, that the Missouri River would be interrupted by a great falls, and then after a short portage, they'd be able to take the Columbia River to the west and the Pacific. Their first glimpse of the

Rocky Mountains hadn't shaken their resolve, though the mountains were perhaps larger and more impressive than they might have expected. And the falls—why, they couldn't be so bad. Here was the real conundrum that the Indians hadn't explained to them: which river to take at the fork. Lewis was dismayed at the lack of information given them. He said of the Mandans' information:

> *what astonishes us a little is that the Indians who*
> *appeared to be so well acquainted with the geography*
> *of this country should not have mentioned this river*
> *on wright hand if it be not the Missouri;* the river
> that scolds all others*, as they call it if there is in*
> *reallity such an one, ought agreeably to their account,*
> *to have fallen in a considerable distance below and*
> *on the other hand if this right hand or N. fork be*
> *the Missouri I am equally astonished at their not*
> *mentioning the S. fork which they must have passed in*
> *order to get to those large falls which they mention on*
> *the Missouri. thus have our cogitating faculties been*
> *busily employed all day.*

When faced with an impasse, the captains did the logical thing. They had everyone stop and make camp—and then they experimented: First, they sent two canoes, one north and one south, for a report on the character of each river. Then, they measured the rivers' widths and depths and described their characters. Finally, as the men were sitting about the campfires, dressing elk skins and making new clothing and moccasins, they took an informal poll.

Nearly every man around the campfire believed that the north fork was the Missouri River. The canoe party that went up reported that it was an easily navigable stream that seemed most like the Missouri. The canoe party that went south reported that at its shallowest the river was six feet deep. But both Lewis and Clark persisted in their belief that the south fork was the Missouri. And they formed two more parties for the investigation, sending a second wave of explorers to test the waters.

When these canoes returned from their respective side trips, the captains met and made another leadership decision. In spite of the popular opinion, they named the north fork the Marias on Saturday, June 8, and prepared to proceed down the south river. The Great Falls would be in their sights and hearing shortly.

# THE GREAT FALLS

## June 13, 1805

Meriwether Lewis was worried. His scouting mission had told him two things: First, this was going to be a long portage. And, second, this was going to be a difficult portage. It was impossible to see how he might move the men, all their canoes, and all their equipment and supplies over the land on the north side of the Missouri. To the south it merely looked impassable, but he was pinning his hopes on making the eighteen-mile trudge around the Great Falls of the Missouri on that side of the river.

A few days after choosing to head south at the fork of what they now called the Marias River and the Missouri, Lewis confirmed the captains' decision to follow that branch. He set off with Gibson and Drouillard and their hunting rifles to scout forward—perhaps to confirm his beliefs once and for all. After about fifteen miles, he heard it: the distinct rumbling rush of water as it cascaded down over chains of rocks in the speeding currents of a river. He had come to the Great Falls.

After penning a description in his journal, Lewis admitted that he was loath to compare his meager words with the grandness of the sight before him when he beheld the falls. He admitted, "I retired to the shade of a tree where I determined to fix my camp for the present and dispatch a man in the morning to inform Capt. C. and the party of my success in finding the falls and settle in their minds all further doubts as to the Missouri."

But that satisfaction must have paled in comparison with the daunting task that he now saw ahead. Their canoes could not hope to navigate the drop of the water—in some places as much as eighty feet from top to crashing bottom. And the rapids were impassable. On the north bank there was no practical way around the great rush of water, so he returned to the rest of camp to report his findings and send out a party to the south.

Meanwhile, Sacagawea had grown very ill, and Clark was attempting to treat her by bleeding, a common remedy of the day. Lewis expressed his distress on seeing her—she was their best hope for trading for horses for the climb across the Rocky Mountains. He set about finding a way to ease her distress and save her life as the scouts were out looking for a way around the falls.

When they returned at dusk on the night of June 16, the report from the scouts was grim. No good portage could be found on the south side of the river either. Ravines and small creeks caused fissures in the ground that made carrying their heavy boats impracticable. They would have to leave the white pirogue—just as they had left the red at the Marias River—and continue on with only their smaller dugout canoes. And they would have to find some way of getting around these Great Falls—sixteen miles in all—with their equipment, supplies, and a means of continuing down the river to its headwaters.

But through some miracle Lewis turned out to have all the answers. He healed Sacagawea by having her drink from the waters of a sulphurous spring. And he had the men cut down young cotton-woods to make wheels to convert the canoes into wagons. They would drag them with their cargo around the Great Falls—and Sacagawea would be well enough to walk with them on the two-week ordeal. A month after seeing the crash of the water for the first time—well past the time when Lewis and Clark had expected to be beyond the shining mountains—they put their boats in the Missouri again and set out for the headwaters. The preparations and portage had taken their toll, but the expedition remained undaunted.

# INDEPENDENCE AND IRON BOATS

## July 4-9, 1805

For weeks Lewis had been agonizing over the delays in travel and in killing the elk necessary to create elk robes to test his prize invention. In addition to the buckskins that the men had cured and sewn into garments for themselves, they were making a skin for an amazing, collapsible iron boat that Lewis planned to set afloat as soon as they breached the portage of the Great Falls.

The boat was a pet project that had been taking up valuable cargo space, and energy to move it, since St. Louis. The idea was that when assembled, the collapsible frame would be covered with the cured elk skins and would float as easily as a canoe. Lewis was proud of the invention and eager to try it out.

By the Fourth of July 1805, the captains and their crew had been at the Great Falls for more than two weeks, negotiating the arduous portage of canoes, baggage, and personnel around the treacherous waters of the Missouri River that tumbled over five waterfalls and their high embankments. They had abandoned the red pirogue near the Marias River, and now the white pirogue had to be left behind, as well. The iron boat would be a useful receptacle for the company's goods and their transportation to the headwaters of the Missouri, where they hoped to meet up with Sacagawea's tribe to trade for horses to carry them across the mountains.

All day on July 4, the men continued their laborious efforts to move the heavily laden canoes across the ground to a safe launching place. And Lewis continued the work on his boat. By the holiday, the skins were in place, and he put the sealing coat on to make it float. It would be a large boat that would carry a great deal of supplies—but it would not require extraordinary effort to move it out of the water. As the men finished their labors on the twenty-ninth birthday of their young nation, the skin was drying by the fire.

To celebrate Independence Day the men rested from their labors and had a dance and fine meal. Cruzatte played the fiddle, and the men capered about after their dinner of bacon, beans, dumplings, and buffalo until their party was interrupted by a natural fireworks display—a thunderstorm. Still, the merriment went on into the night, flavored by a bit of whiskey and tempered by the knowledge that it was the last of the supply.

On July 9 preparations continued to get the party underway and in the water again. Lewis was delighted when his iron boat floated "like a cork," when she was put in the river. But after only a few minutes, the boat leaked and came apart at the seams. Dismayed at the failure of his pet invention, he directed that she be put to rest along shore. The many pounds of iron that they had hauled so many miles were of no use to them now. They were short of room for supplies and personnel as they continued down the Missouri.

What happened to Lewis's invention is one of the great mysteries of the expedition. Archaeologists and historians have searched for its remains along the Missouri River, but no trace has ever been found.

# THE GATES OF THE MOUNTAINS

## July 19, 1805

It was such a relief to be back on the river! After the agonies of the two-week-long portage around the Great Falls, the Corps of Discovery was moving quickly toward the headwaters of the Missouri River. Preparations for the portage had taken longer than they expected, and even with the ingenious wheels they used to roll their canoes on the ground near the river, the experience had been grueling. Lewis's iron boat had been buried in a cache near the river long enough ago that they barely noticed its departure from their ranks any longer— except that the weight they were carrying was that much less in the new dugout canoes. Now, the headwaters were near, and the scenery continued to be breathtaking as they entered a deep gash in the earth made by the river's passage over time.

As usual, the captains split up their duties for the day. Lewis was riding in one of the canoes, while Clark was passing by on foot on the trails above the river canyon. Clark's journal entries are of the rocky ground and the prickly pear needles that he pulled from his tender feet. But Lewis was rushing agreeably on below.

The current of the river was strong, and on either side of the boats, the walls of the canyon were imposingly steep. Where sunlight penetrated, the layers of rocky walls were gold, green, and brown. And ahead of the boats, the river seemed to divide the very face of the mountain in two as it pushed its way through.

Lewis wrote his journal entry in a camp on a narrow shore ensconced in the deep canyon, which was dark before the usual hour because of its shadowy depths. In his journal entry he waxed poetic about the scenery all about him and named the gap in the river, "The Gates of the Mountains." Today, visitors can follow the route of the expedition through the canyon and picnic at the very spot where Lewis composed his journal entry.

# MUSQUITERS

## July 25, 1805

As the end of July 1805 approached, the Corps of Discovery was nearing the Three Forks of the Missouri River and the headwaters of the river that had carried them so far on their journey. The mountains all around were high and rocky and the plains in between studded with prickly pear cactus and tall grass. Along the banks of the river, the land was lightly wooded and game was plentiful, but the men were the game for the small, noisome, winged insects that plagued them all. Mosquitoes infested the bottomlands along the Missouri River, and the entries in the captains' journals. Clark had nearly as many spellings for the creatures' name as swollen bites on his ankles.

When the small band of mountain men, Sacagawea, and little Pomp—her son—reached the Three Forks, many of their troubles were behind them. They'd made their way through land inhabited by the great white bear and learned to deal with the carnivore. They'd eaten well from the bounty of the land: game, as well as roots, berries, and fish. Even the portage of the Great Falls was past, and Sacagawea was beginning to recognize landmarks around her. This was her childhood home, and it was the object of the expedition to meet up with her people to trade for horses to cross the Rocky Mountains.

Complaints about the cactus and the insects were many as they crossed the valley on the Jefferson River, named by Lewis and Clark for the originator of their expedition. (They had also named the other two forks for expedition benefactors: Madison for the vice president and Gallatin for the secretary of the treasury.) But hopes were high for a quick crossing of the mountains and meeting up with the Columbia River. Even though the portaging of the Great Falls had taken so much of the summer, surely they could make up the time in the mountain crossing.

But as the prickly pear and the mosquito, small as they were, wore on the spirits of the men as they soldiered forward, they began to despair of finding Sacagawea's people and trading for the necessary horses. And more hardships lay before them than behind them as the mosquitoes buzzed around their heads.

# A FAMILY REUNION

## August 17, 1805

Sacagawea could not contain her joy. She danced from foot to foot and sucked her fingers with the excitement of a small child. Clark finally understood. They had reached the Shoshone—her birth people. This was their village. The hope was that Lewis would be here, too.

A week before, Sacagawea had taught Lewis the word, *ta-vai-bon-e*, or possibly *tab-ta-bone*, as he set off to look for the Shoshone, who would have horses to trade for the journey over the Rocky Mountains. Lewis thought it was the word for "white man," but it was actually the word for "stranger." The Shoshone had never seen whites before, and they had no word to describe them.

Lewis's plan was to walk ahead with a small group to find the Shoshone, while the rest of the party waited to catch up. He first spotted a lone Shoshone man on August 11, but in spite of waving his blanket in the sign of friendship and calling out the word that Sacagawea had taught him, the man vanished.

The Shoshone may have believed that Lewis and the few men with him were members of a Blackfoot raiding party. The Shoshone were starving—they didn't have enough food to support themselves through the winter, and the fierce Blackfeet were their mortal enemies. On August 13, when Lewis finally met Shoshone who didn't flee in alarm, the exchanging of gifts led to many embraces by the Shoshone, and by the time the rest of the party caught up, he would say he was "heartily tired of the national hug."

When Sacagawea came into the camp, Clark and the other members of the party also shared in the "national hug." But Sacagawea had even greater joy in store for her. Almost immediately, she recognized a woman who had been taken prisoner with her as a little girl, but who had escaped from the Minetarees. She couldn't believe that her friend had made it back to their people alive!

But the object of the meeting with the Shoshone was not fond reunions. Sacagawea was brought to the council of Lewis and Clark and the chiefs of the Shoshone to talk about trading for the valuable horses that the party needed to make their way across the mountains.

It was unusual for a woman to come into the council to speak, so Sacagawea had her blanket wrapped around her and her eyes cast downward as she began her translation. Lewis spoke his words in English, a translator named LaBiche said them in French to Charbonneau, he said them in turn in Hidatsa to Sacagawea, and then she spoke in the language of her childhood. After a moment the reply came, and Sacagawea leapt to her feet. The voice of the young chief, Cameahwait, was the voice of her own clan brother. She ran to him with her blanket and embraced him in its folds.

The trading with the Shoshone was successful, and for Sacagawea the trip must have been successful for more reasons. The intervening years since her capture had been difficult for the Shoshone, and her parents and sisters were dead. But she became the adoptive mother of her sister's son, as was the custom of the Shoshone. Though she had to leave her newly adopted son and her clan brother behind as the expedition traveled on to the Pacific, Sacagawea had enjoyed an astonishing reunion with her family.

# TRAVELER'S REST

## September 9, 1805

After months of only their own company on the vast plains of the Louisiana Territory, finally the Corps of Discovery was in the mountains and had contact with the Shoshone and the Flathead tribes. Now they had only to cross those mountains and make their way to the Pacific Ocean to complete their western journey.

As usual, the captains were after something from the tribes they met along the way: information. They had no map to guide them across those mountains and only the hearsay of travelers—told through multiple translations—to show them the way. So far, that information had proven less than accurate. The falls of the Missouri had taken them two weeks to portage, not three days, as they had anticipated, and preparing to get back on the river had required more time. And now the mountains that were supposed to take them only a day to cross surrounded them on all sides. The mountains in front of them—the Bitterroots—were the worst ones, yet.

On September 9, 1805, after two days with little food and the mountains yet ahead of them, Lewis called for a rest. They made camp beneath the formidable snow-covered peaks on a little creek, and the next morning Lewis sent out all of the hunters to procure food for their mountain crossing. An old Indian, called Old Toby, offered them information: He told them to head up the creek and cross the mountains—the same formidable peaks that were darkening their campground.

That day, they were joined by a group of Indians who were in pursuit of stolen horses. Because they had come from the west, it made it seem possible, after all, that the mountains could be crossed. And best of all, they offered the news that it was only six or seven sleeps to the big water: the Pacific Ocean.

The other news that Old Toby gave them at the place they called Traveler's Rest was this: If they'd followed the Clark Fork River from the Missouri instead of following the Missouri to its headwaters, they would have saved seven weeks in their crossing to the big mountains, where food shortages and snow made their crossing risky. And they now knew they couldn't get back home before the winter set in.

# NOT EVEN THEIR WOOD

## October 13–14, 1805

Fall had crept into the air by the time the Corps of Discovery made their way to the Snake River. At last, they were across the Rocky Mountains and back on a water passage to the Pacific Ocean. Soon, they would meet up with the Columbia River and make their way quickly to the sea for the winter.

Though the prairies east of the Rocky Mountains had been virtually empty of people, the lands surrounding the Snake River teemed with them. Clark attributed their friendliness to the presence of Sacagawea and Pomp in their midst. He thought that having a woman along signified their peaceful intentions. Everyone, it seemed, wanted to trade with the whites as they made their way down the river, offering dried salmon and dogs in exchange for trade goods.

In truth it's possible that the tribes of the Pacific Northwest were simply more used to whites. British and Russian traders and trappers had been making their way to the West Coast of North America for many years and had set up trading forts and other lines of trade with the native people there. The whites carried goods that were not available in any other way, even if some of them were the worthless medals with the picture of Jefferson on one side.

Clark was particularly admiring of the people they encountered, though both of the captains were very interested in the lives that the native people of the Pacific coast lived. They recorded many details about native languages and customs in their journal.

In this aspect of their journey, the Corps of Discovery was utterly successful. They had managed to establish peaceful trade with many of the tribes along their route. Even though they had determined that there was no all-water route to the Pacific, and it was clear that their route to the Pacific was not the shortest overland route, they had accomplished much. Clark wrote in his journal, "we have made it a point at all times not to take any thing belonging to the Indians even their wood." But even the captains' enlightened policies toward the native peoples of the Pacific Northwest could not change the fact that their way of life was about to be forever altered by whites.

# THE DALLES

## October 24, 1805

Extra care for the safety of the men was the order of the day. Rumors of a planned attack against their little band had reached the captains' ears as they descended the Columbia River. Now, they were at a point in the river that Clark described as, "agitated in a most Shocking manner."

On October 24, 1805, having come out of the mountains, heading down the river, the Corps of Discovery was still a month away from the Pacific Ocean. To retreat to the mountains was unthinkable; to lose a man was a worse thought, yet. They had to proceed with caution.

While the river roiled and the rumors boiled around them, a break was in order. The men made camp on the shore of the Columbia River above the rapids—the long narrows of the treacherous passage now known as the Dalles. They would have to traverse the rapids either by running them in the canoes or by portaging around them. It was time for planning and careful movement.

The Nez Perce guides that had accompanied the expedition over the mountains declared that they would go no farther at the short narrows, the first of the dangerous rapids. They claimed that the Nez Perce were at war with the Wishram Indians in the area, and they could not enter enemy territory. As a mandate of the expedition, Lewis and Clark were expected to help make peace between tribes in order to ease trade relations, so they convinced the reluctant Nez Perce to stay for two days while they negotiated a peace.

Two days later, a settlement was reached, and Cruzatte played his fiddle as the Nez Perce and the Wishram celebrated with the men, but in the morning as they prepared to mount their boats again, the mood was somber. Lining the shore were the men who were too fearful to be in the small canoes, and in the boats were the finest oarsmen of the bunch. They had to run the rapids; the men on shore held lifelines that they were ready to throw at the first sign of danger. Others held the guns and important papers. This was a dangerous business.

At the end of the day, all of the boats had made it safely through the narrows and into calmer waters. Surely, the worst was behind them, and they'd soon arrive at the Pacific Ocean.

# TAKING A VOTE

## November 24, 1805

At last, the expedition had reached the Pacific Ocean. Its booming had grown louder as they came near the mouth of the Columbia River, and the excitement over seeing its water grew daily. The object of their journey was at hand. Even though they had not found a water route across the country, joy was in the air.

Soon, however, their thoughts turned to surviving the impending winter. The cold rains of the Pacific Northwest were upon them, and turning back to the mountains was not an option. The expedition needed supplies, and its people needed rest. And their most immediate need was for food and shelter. If they stayed where they were, then a trading ship might come to the coast, and they could resupply.

The Indians here knew of white men, and they were shrewd traders. The beads, medals, and trinkets that Lewis and Clark had were of little interest to them, and they would only trade for rotten, old salmon, not the fresh meat that the expedition members needed.

For the second time during the expedition, the captains took a vote. But for the first time, York, Clark's slave, and Sacagawea, the Shoshone wife of Charbonneau, had a vote. Clark carefully recorded the opinions of the men. The two choices were to cross over the river to where the local Indians said there was game to be had or to stay put on the shore of the Pacific Ocean. Each man voiced his preference—and so did Sacagawea. She said she wanted to go where there were plenty of "potas" to dig, the wappato roots that could be eaten like potatoes all winter long.

The day after the vote, Lewis took a scouting group across the great river to see the spot the Indians had pointed out to them. It was marshy, heavily treed, and wet. But there were creeks for water, plenty of elk, and nearby they could have a saltworks. They decided on a location for Fort Clatsop, and the party got ready to move.

Eventually, although the presence of game was certainly a boon for the ragged group, the wet and the rain of Fort Clatsop caused a disappointment. Their clothes rotted off their bodies, and the cold and damp in the small log enclosure was nearly unbearable. The winter was a long, hard one—full of work to replenish their stores as best they could and the anticipation of the journey home.

According to some historians, a trading ship may have visited the coast during the winter of 1805–1806, but Lewis and Clark never knew about it. If true, it made no difference to the expedition. For whatever reason, the Indians who would have been aware of the traders' arrival never told the ship's captain of the band of whites camped nearby, and they didn't tell Lewis and Clark about the arrival of the traders.

# CHRISTMAS ON THE PACIFIC

## December 25, 1805

Shouts and gunshots roused the captains from their slumber in their dark quarters at Fort Clatsop. It was not alarm, but joy, that had made early risers of the men and inspired a celebratory mood that morning. Even on the Pacific coast, far from home and loved ones, it was Christmas.

Clark wrote later that day in his journal,

> *after brackfast we divided our Tobacco which amounted to 12 carrots one half of which we gave to the men of the party who used tobacco, and to those who doe not use it we make a present of a handkerchief. . . . I recved a pres[e]nt of Capt. L. of a fleece hosrie Shirt Draws and Socks, a pr. Mockersons of Whitehouse a Small Indian basket of Gutherich, two Dozen white weazils tails of the Indian woman, & some black root of the Indians before their departure.*

It was to be the last Christmas the men spent away from home, and they were cheerful throughout the day in spite of the wet, unpleasant weather from which they could never escape at Fort Clatsop, and they gave what they had to each other. It was in stark contrast even to the Christmas with the Mandans the year before, when most of their hardship was ahead of them and stores of tobacco and whiskey were more plentiful. Now, they had no whiskey at all, but the spirit of Christmas seemed to pervade the dark log buildings tucked into the swampy woods of the Pacific coast.

They were unlucky in the weather, and in one other aspect, as well. Even though the spirit of generosity had prevailed—even from Sacagawea, who was almost definitely not a Christian and was unfamiliar with the customs of the white man's feast days—it was in "feasting" that their day was entirely a disappointment. Clark wrote,

> *we would have Spent this day the nativity of Christ in*
> *feasting, had we any thing either to raise our Sperits or*
> *even gratify our appetites, our Diner concisted of pore*
> *Elk, so much Spoiled that we eate it thro' mear necessity,*
> *Some Spoiled pounded fish and a fiew roots.*

# THE WHALE

## January 5, 1806

Fort Clatsop was cold and wet. It was always cold and wet, and even the Christmas celebration ten days before had not helped the men's dampened spirits. They had made it all the way to the Pacific coast, but there was no "Northwest Passage" on water to make trade there easier. Spring and the return to the Great Plains and then home couldn't come soon enough for the explorers. But good news was about to arrive.

The expedition had run out of salt, and without it the unvarying diet of elk meat and roots had become even less palatable than usual. A detail had been formed to set up a saltworks on the Pacific, and Privates Willard and Wiser had come back to report on their progress.

The saltworks, set up about fifteen miles from Fort Clatsop, was producing nearly a gallon a day. Lewis was beside himself with excitement. He had been craving salt since it had run out a month before. But Clark was far more excited by the other news that Willard and Wiser brought back from the coast.

The salt-makers had been given a present of meat by the Killa-muck Indians, who lived near the saltworks. But it wasn't just elk or beaver or dog—not even salmon. It was whale blubber.

Lewis wrote of the blubber in his journal: "it was white & not unlike the fat of Poork, tho' the texture was more spongey and some-what coarser. I had a part of it cooked and found it very pallitable and tender, it resembled the beaver or the dog in flavour."

But while Lewis was momentarily engaged in culinary criticism, Clark was fascinated by the idea of the whale itself. It turned out that he was not the only one. The next day, Lewis wrote:

> *Capt Clark set out after an early breakfast with the party in two canoes as had been concerted the last evening; Charbono and his Indian woman were also of the party; the Indian woman was very impotunate to be permitted to go, and was therefore indulged; she observed that she had traveled a long way with us to see the great waters, and that now that monstrous fish was also to be seen, she thought it very hard she could not be permitted to see either (she had never yet been to the Ocean).*

We can't know what Sacagawea thought when she finally did see the ocean and the great fish washed up on shore, but it must have been an amazing sight for all of the expedition members, with the waves crashing around the now bare and bleached bones of the whale on the beach. Clark had been in hopes of trading for blubber—but the local Tillamooks, who were already boiling the blubber for oil—were at first uninterested. Finally, they changed their minds.

The three hundred pounds that they eventually agreed to trade fed the expedition for three weeks and must have raised spirits.

Clark wrote in his journal, thanking "providence for . . . having Sent this monster to be Swallowed by us in Sted of Swallowing us as jonah's did."

It was a welcome interlude in the circus of damp and fleas and work—for the expedition had much to do to prepare for its return journey—and it would certainly have been unfair for Sacagawea to have gone so far and not seen the ocean or the great fish.

# BUYING HATS

## February 22, 1806

The long winter at Fort Clatsop wore on, and the members of the Corps of Discovery found themselves with much to do. Gibson, Bratton, Ordway, Willard, and McNeal had been ill but were recovering. One of the canoes slipped away with the tide and had to be brought back by Sergeant Pryor. And each day slipped into the next. The men were occupied with keeping dry and staying warm, preparing moccasins and clothing for the long return trip in the spring, and staving off boredom.

As with their winter camp on the Missouri, the Corps of Discovery had near neighbors while waiting at Fort Clatsop—the tribal namesake of their tiny settlement in the swampy woods. Trade with the Clatsop provided entertainment and quality goods and services throughout the winter.

Captain Lewis remarked on the skills of the local Indians, "the woodwork and sculpture of these people as well as these hats and their waterproof baskets evince an ingenuity by no means common among the Aborigenes of America."

He and Clark were well pleased at the delivery of cedar bark hats that they'd ordered from some Clatsop women. The hats were plumed with tufts of the tall, reedy bear grass, its bushy tail providing ornament. They were so pleased, in fact, that Clatsop hats were purchased for the whole party—useful items to be sure because the men spent so much time in the hot sun, but the first tourist sales in the Pacific Northwest, as well.

Food and horses also passed between the Clatsop and the Corps of Discovery all winter. And more than once, the Clatsop drove a hard bargain for their goods or services. But they were welcome company, and they provided necessities to the men in Fort Clatsop that long, cold, wet winter.

# THE RETURN BEGINS

## March 18, 1806

Rain showers fell frequently on Fort Clatsop as the men of the Corps of Discovery began their preparations for the long trip back to St. Louis. All the long, wet winter, men had been ill, and now as all hands were needed for the departure, several complained of sickness. Drouillard was laid up with a pain in his side that must have frightened the men after the death of Sergeant Floyd from appendicitis early in the expedition.

But it was time for the journey to begin. Canoes had to be caulked and waterproofed, supplies of food prepared and packed, moccasins repaired, and clothing made. Trading with the Clatsops involved a flurry of last-minute negotiations, and then it was time for the expedition to depart.

The Clatsops and other coastal Indians were used to trading with whites, but most of their encounters were with traders who had come from the big waters, not from the furiously rolling Columbia River. Russian and English traders had been visiting them for years, and the goods they exchanged had made their way into the lives of the Clatsop.

In fact one hope of the captains had been that they might meet up with one of those trading ships over the winter. Then, they could send goods, perhaps a few men, and—most importantly—news of their success to President Jefferson. As the end of March neared, however, such contact seemed unlikely. All of the men and their belongings must go back the way they had come: in the canoes, on horseback, and on foot up the river, over the mountains, and across the plains to the Missouri before returning to St. Louis.

Before turning their canoes up the Columbia, however, Lewis and Clark had one last request of the friendly Clatsops who had attended them throughout the winter. They left a list of the names of their party with the following statement behind, for other parties coming from the Pacific to see, though it probably never found its way to its intended recipients.

> *The object of this list is, that through the medium of some civilized person who may see the same, it may be made known to the informed world, that the party consisting of the persons whose names are hereunto annexed, and who were sent out by the government of the U'States in May 1804. to explore the interior of the Continent of North America, did penetrate the same by way of the Missouri and Columbia Rivers, to the discharge of the latter into the Pacific Ocean, where they arrived on the 14th of November 1805, and from whence they departed the day of March 1806 on their return to the United States by the same rout they had come out.*

# MAGIC FOR WAPPATO

## April 2, 1806

As the Corps of Discovery made its way up the mighty Columbia River, the news from the Indians they passed was not good. Food was scarce, and they didn't expect the salmon run for another month. And even if they had had food to trade, these Indians were savvy from years of trading with the whites who visited their villages in search of rich furs and fish. They weren't going to take simple beads and medals in exchange for their precious foodstuffs.

Lewis and Clark looked about them in the fertile valley and knew that their claims of hunger were valid. Elk and deer did not fill the shores of the river as they did elsewhere in the vast country they'd explored. Without salmon in the river, food would be scarce, indeed. The danger of moving on was evident: not enough food to fuel the men in the labor involved in pushing the canoe upstream. The danger of staying put took a longer view to discover: The water of the Missouri might freeze before they could travel down to St. Louis by fall, which would mean another winter away from home.

Trading, always important to the band of buckskin- and moccasin-clad explorers, took on as much urgency as it had when they were in pursuit of Shoshone horses for use in crossing the Rocky Mountains in the fall of 1805. Lewis and Clark made a decision: They would stay put until they had traded for enough dried meat to take them as far as the Chopunnish village and the possibility of more trade.

Trade made up most of Captain Lewis's thoughts on April 2, 1806, as he planned out their trip to the east and home:

> to exchange our perogues for canoes with the natives on our way to the great falls of the columbia or purchase such canoes from them for Elk-skins and Merchandize as would answer our purposes. these canoes we intend exchanging with the natives of the plains for horses as we proceed untill we obtain as many as will enable us to travel altogether by land. at some convenient point, perhaps at the entrence of the S.E. branch, we purpose sending a party of four or five men ahead to collect our horses that they may be in readiness for us by rival at the Chopunnish; calculating by thus acquiring a large stock of horses we shall not only secure the means of tranpoorting our baggage over the mountains but that we will also have provided the means of subsisting; for we now view the horses as our only certain resource for food, nor do we look forward to it with any detestation or horrow, so soon is the mind which is occupied with any interesting object, reconciled to it's situation.

While Lewis laid his plans, Clark set out with a small party to explore a river that the Native Americans called the Mult-no-mah, which is now called the Willamette. Along the river he passed a village and stopped in hopes of trading with the Indians there—whom he called the Ne-cha-co-lee—for the wappato root that had sustained them throughout the winter at Fort Clatsop.

Clark reported that the people in the house he visited were, "sulkey and positively refused to sell any."

But Clark was persistent. He would not go away without the roots. First, he lit a fuse that he carried in his pocket and threw it into the fire—causing a great spectacle when the flames changed colors and burned wildly. Next, he used a magnet to make the needle on his compass spin rapidly and so alarmed the Ne-cha-co-lee with his antics that they put all the wappato they could carry on the ground by his feet.

Clark reported, "I lit my pipe and gave them smoke, & gave the womin the full amount [value] of the roots which they had out at my feet. they appeared somewhat passified and I left them and proceeded on."

A few days later, the party moved again as a group up the Columbia River, and Clark's skills were called into action once more. The small band—always looking for a trade and to extend its mandate of creating peaceful relations between the Great White Fathers in Washington and the tribes of the Louisiana Territory—paused beside the Columbia River with the Chopunnish Indians. They sat in council for several days, making treaties between the tribes and sealing their own relations. And then word passed among them that Clark could cure ailments of the eye.

On the morning of May 12, 1806, Clark ate breakfast and administered "eye water" to almost forty patients. He commented that the ailments of the Chopunnish were probably related to their all-root diet and noted the complaints of rheumatism and eye disease among them.

As a result of the goodwill he created, they sat down at a grand council during the day. The Native Americans told the band that they had listened to all of its advice and would follow it precisely. It was a victory for the peacekeeping mission of the expedition. And Clark basked in its glow—until he was called away to administer more eye water.

But in spite of all their efforts on the Columbia, soon they would face the Rocky Mountains again, low on food and deep in snow.

# POMP'S ILLNESS

## May 26, 1806

The little boy had made it across the country, from the Missouri River home of his mother's adopted people and the little fort, inhabited by the white men, where he was born, to the mighty Pacific Ocean. Those white men had become the traveling companions of little Jean Baptiste Charbonneau and his mother, Sacagawea. And now he was a beloved member of the expedition.

He was just over a year old when the expedition headed back up the Columbia River to return to the place of his birth. Food had been scarce as they made their way east and north, and many of the men were sick and tired from the long winter's confinement and the new hardships on the river as they moved slowly toward home. Jean Baptiste—fondly called Pomp or Pompey by the men and his mother—was now ill, as well.

Snow and rain had been falling on the men in their tents and on the ground as they struggled to keep warm and comfortable in their temporary camp. They could not enter the Rocky Mountains and continue their way toward home, as the snow still lay too deep. On

May 21 they were wet, cold, and miserable, and they had eaten the last of their meat and expected no more food from the locals—for they had little left to trade, and these Indians were too sophisticated to simply take the shiny buttons from uniform coats in exchange for roots and meat.

On May 22 the sun shone brighter, and their belongings began to dry out in the warm sun. The captains ordered a colt killed for meat, and fishermen found fish in the river. But the news was not all good. Clark reported in his journal: "Shabonos son a small child is dangerously ill. his jaw and throat is much swelled. we apply a poltice of onions, after giveing him some creem of tarter &c."

Small children were especially susceptible to illness at the time when Lewis and Clark crossed the country—vaccines were in the distant future and even an understanding of germs and bacteria was yet to come. In some ways it was a wonder that Pomp was not ill more often as he traveled with the men across the country. He was very ill at the end of May 1806, and the captains and his parents, as well as the rest of the crew, must have despaired for him.

They treated him with cream of tartar, hardly an effective antibiotic, and by making poultices out of the wild onions that grew in the area, heating the pungent herbs and applying them to his swollen neck. For days this treatment continued, and one or the other of the captains remarked on his progress in his journal nearly every day.

Finally, on June 3 Clark made the report: Their invalid was on the mend. And none too soon. They would enter the Rocky Mountains shortly and begin the next arduous part of their journey.

The men must have been relieved at the recovery of their small companion and mascot—perhaps mostly Captain Clark, who at the end of the journey would offer to adopt young Pomp and raise him as his own.

# A BRIEF RETREAT

## June 17, 1806

The horses struggled across the rapidly flowing creek. It had been a dangerous crossing after two days of struggling through the snow. It was spring in the lowlands, but the Corps of Discovery had been moving upward into the depths of winter as they moved into the Rocky Mountains. The run-off from melting snow was fueling the creek, but there were still plenty of the white leavings of winter around them as they attempted to push on.

After a month of waiting, the Corps of Discovery was trying to move forward on their return trip. They'd been warned of deep snow in the mountains when they reached the foothills in the middle of May, and they had prudently paused and waited for warm weather to come.

On June 15 they moved out of camp in a driving rain, slipping along the rocky paths into the mountains on their horses. By June 16 they could see that in the woods around them snow was still almost four feet deep in places. They went farther, the horses traveling over and through the snow. On June 17 they crossed the rushing creek, and Lewis and Clark sat down to consider their actions.

Food was still a problem in the mountains, as the hunters had found no game for many weeks, and roots and meat from butchered horses wouldn't hold out forever. The expedition's policy of living off the land as they traveled wouldn't sustain them unless they made it to good fishing or hunting soon.

Clark remarked that his hands and feet were cold and numb from the frigid air around them. A dunking in the creek would have had serious consequences for the man, his horse, and the equipment he was carrying, so an alternate route around the creek crossings was scouted. But both Lewis and Clark soon realized the futility of their march. Clark recorded in his journal:

> *if we proceeded and Should git bewildered in those Mountains the certainty was that we Should lose all of our horses and consequently our baggage enstrements perhaps our papers and thus eventually resque the loss of our discoveries which we had already made if we should be so fortunate as to escape with life.*

Reluctantly, the captains concluded that they could not proceed through these mountains in the snow without a knowledgeable guide to help them find their way and find food for themselves and their horses. They built scaffolding and unloaded their equipment onto it, covering it well—and they marked its location so that they could retrieve it—and then they turned the horses around to search for a guide before proceeding in the deep snow. Clark sadly noted in his journal: "this is the first time since we have been on this tour that we have ever been compelled to retreat or make a retragrade march."

# FIREWORKS

## June 25, 1806

George Drouillard and George Shannon had set off from the expedition on June 18 to negotiate with Native American guides after the setback of late snow in the mountains had so disheartened the Corps of Discovery. Captain Clark reported that they carried with them a rifle, "which we offered as a reward to any of them who would engage to conduct us to Clarks river at the entrance of Travellers rest Creek." The setback and retreat had dismayed the men, and the tone of Clark's words about inducing help rang with need.

In Clark's journal of June 19, however, the tone changed. Even though Potts cut his leg and Colter's horse tumbled with him into a creek, the game and fish were abundant, if difficult to obtain, and the campsite was pleasant, even though the "musquetors" were again troublesome. Then, on the 20th, Clark's tone changed again. Faced with the prospect of waiting for another few days for the return of Drouillard and Shannon, the difficulties of hunting and fishing dragged him down again. He laid out detailed plans for how the party could proceed, with or without help, to move out of the mountains.

By the night of the 22nd, Drouillard and Shannon still had not returned, but two Indians arrived in camp and the captains were determined to secure their services to help them to Traveler's Rest. Late in the afternoon of the 23rd, the two men arrived in camp with three guides who were willing to help the party reach the Missouri River in exchange for two guns. On the morning of the 24th, the Corps of Discovery was once more on the move. Horses collected, they began making their way out of the mountains.

That night, the corps put their troubles behind them. Clark wrote on June 15, "last evening the indians entertained us with setting the fir trees on fire." Camped near a stand of the highly inflammable Alpine fir, the guides stacked dry limbs around the bottoms of the trees and set them alight, sending flame shooting from the bottom to the top of the tree. Clark described the spectacle: "this exhibition reminded me of a display of fireworks."

The act of the fire was a charm of sorts, intended to bring good luck and good weather for the journey out of the mountains. Hardship and worry were still ahead, but the days of worry and retreat were over for the moment.

# A HOT BATH AT LAST

# June 29, 1806

The water bubbled warm and inviting out of the ground. Soon, the men were luxuriating in the hot, clean water and shaking off the cold and hunger of the past few days. Crossing the Rocky Mountains for the second time had been an ordeal that none would soon forget.

It had seemed like summer when the expedition, eager to be home and to share the insights of their adventure, had turned toward the Bitterroot Mountains at the beginning of June. The air was finally warm, and signs of spring were everywhere in the vegetation. They couldn't understand why, even on June 10, the Nez Perce warned them to wait another month before entering the mountains. The experienced natives claimed that the snows would not have receded from the steep slopes yet, but the expedition was eager to press on.

For five days they rested with impatience in the low country, and that was enough.

On June 17, as they struggled through the snow with the knowledge that there would be no food for their horses or possibly for themselves, they were forced to turn back.

Injuries, cold, and mosquitoes plagued them as they waited for the two Nez Perce who had promised to come as guides to arrive at camp. They were desperately in need of assistance and feared that if they did not cross the mountains soon they would not make it back to the United States in 1806. Another winter with the Mandans must have seemed a heavy hardship to some with the previous winter's deprivations not that far behind and a wintry landscape before them.

Finally, the promised guides arrived and the struggle over the mountains continued with only roots to eat and no salt or oil with which to cook them. The Nez Perce entertained the men with pyrotechnic displays of burning fir trees that reminded them of fireworks, but they must have proved little distraction from the thoughts of getting out of the snowy mountains and finally having something to eat.

It was Sunday, June 29, when they finally reached what is now called Lolo Hot Springs. The men bathed in the springs and enjoyed themselves immensely now that the hardship of crossing the mountains was behind them. Finally, they were in what is now Montana, and it seemed that they were truly heading home.

# SPLITTING UP

## July 3, 1806

With the treacherous snowy mountains behind them and the Great Plains and plenty of game and home before them, the captains had made a decision and worked out a plan. They were eager to return to the states to report on their expedition and sleep in beds and eat bread with butter, but there was still more exploration to be done across what is now Montana.

Captain Lewis wrote in his journal on July 3, 1806: "I took leave of my worthy friend and companion Capt. Clark and the party that accompanyed him. I could not avoid feeling much concern on this occasion although I hoped this seperation was only momentary."

For more than two years, the captains had been in almost constant contact. Even when the parties would split up on the trail, it was only for a day or two, and they would be traveling in the same direction. This time, they would split the whole party in two and go on separate expeditions: Lewis to travel north to explore the upper reaches of the Marias River and Clark to map the Yellowstone River to its mouth at the Missouri.

There were plenty of volunteers for Lewis's northern excursion. Sergeant Patrick Gass and Privates William Werner, Robert Frazer, Joseph Field, Reubin Field, John Thompson, Silas Goodrich, and Hugh McNeal, and interpreter George Drouillard were with him when he pulled out of camp that morning. Thompson, Goodrich, and McNeal were going along as far as the Great Falls, where they would camp and wait for Lewis's other volunteers to return from their explorations and a rendezvous with members of Clark's party.

Clark set out that morning with Sergeant John Ordway, York, and the Charbonneau family, along with the rest of the expedition. They would head down the Beaverhead River to the Three Forks, and then Ordway would lead a group down the Missouri to meet up with Lewis's encamped party at the Great Falls. Never before had the group of hardy adventurers been so spread out across the vast wilderness—and it was natural that it gave Lewis and Clark cause for concern.

There were serious reasons for the diverging of the two parties. They had not located the fabled Northwest Passage, an all-water route to open up trade between the states and the Pacific Northwest. Keeping the British, so recently overthrown, from spreading their influence throughout the West would be simpler with a water route or even an easier overland route to their strongholds on the edge of the Louisiana Territory. Competition from American merchants could stave off that influence.

The expedition members could hardly be blamed for not finding an all-water route, because such a passage did not exist. But they were still in search of an easier overland route. As they turned toward home, Lewis would explore the Marias River and follow an overland shortcut described to him by the Nez Perce in the feeble hope that they could salvage that part of their mission.

The other serious reason for the split was the need for a northern boundary to the Louisiana Purchase. It was decreed by treaty that the northern boundary was at 49º, 37', but no one had ever surveyed that boundary. Lewis would establish a geographic reference point for the end of the territory to the north.

When the Fourth of July came, it was not mentioned in the journals of Lewis or Clark; there was no celebration of their third national holiday on the expedition. Splitting up after all their time together was sobering, not joyous. When the parties reunited at the mouth of the Yellowstone, then there would be stories to tell. It would be six weeks, an altercation with the Blackfeet, and a wounded captain before they met up again.

# THE YELLOWSTONE

# July 15, 1806

Captain Clark's small band was almost giddy with enjoyment. They had no portage across the Great Falls, plenty of horses, fast canoes, and the bounty of the land to depend on for food. The summertime weather was beautiful, and the only flies in the ointment were mosquitoes.

After parting from their companions, who headed north with Lewis to investigate the Marias River and retrieve canoes from their caches on the Missouri, the small group of men, a woman, and a child, descended the Bitterroot Valley and crossed the Big Hole Valley with ease, reaching the supplies and canoes that they had cached the previous August. Most precious among those supplies was tobacco—the sweet, pungent smell filling the air after months of abstinence.

With canoes in working order and supplies to spare, they pushed off down the Jefferson River to the Three Forks. The first day, they traveled ninety-seven glorious miles; the second day passed in bliss as they learned just how much easier their return trip down the river would be; and on the third day, they were at the Three Forks of the

Missouri. The relief of the group was palpable. Filled with sweet thoughts of home, they were making excellent time.

At Three Forks they left their canoes and set out cross-country again. Forty-nine horses of the fine band they'd amassed through clever trading over the previous weeks carried them overland to the Yellowstone—more than enough to supply their needs and even withstand the predations of the Crow Indians, who were eager to get their hands on the fine animals. The rest of the horses, in the charge of Sergeant Pryor, were sent overland to the mouth of the Yellowstone and then on to the Mandan villages for trade.

At the Yellowstone, Clark ordered dugout canoes made from the timber on the shore and set off down the swiftly flowing river. He could see the magnificent mountains of what would become Yellowstone National Park in the distance as they set off, and they continued to speed toward the Missouri River and their rendezvous with the rest of the expedition.

But a few days later, they met up again with Sergeant Pryor, who had lost the rest of the horses to the Crow. He had ingeniously made two bull boats from buffalo skins and floated up the river to meet his commander—sorry for the loss, but perhaps also pleased with his mode of transport.

Other than the loss of horses and the trade goods they represented, Clark's voyage down the Yellowstone would be a raging success. The only false note was recorded for posterity when Lewis summarized Clark's notes in a journal entry. They claimed that the Yellowstone River emptied out near the settlements in New Mexico, and because there were no falls on the Yellowstone River to impede travel, that it might be a viable trade route to explore for Spanish goods. Their journal entries are confusing, and the statements just plain wrong. Even if New Mexico was at the end of the Yellowstone, the massive Tower Fall and Upper and Lower Falls of the Yellowstone would have daunted even the explorers who had made the grand portage around the Great Falls of the Missouri. But nothing could diminish the joy of turning home and finding the swift road of water beneath their boats propelling them forward.

# POMPEY'S PILLAR

## July 25, 1806

Captain Clark stood at the top of the sandstone monolith and joyfully shouted down at his companions. The last few days of travel, as they cruised along the swiftly moving Yellowstone River in dugout canoes, had been some of the best of the expedition. Even the mosquitoes had seemed less bothersome because they were now near the spot where they would reunite with their companions and because they were truly headed east—toward home.

It had been more than a year since the small band of explorers had left the Mandan villages in North Dakota as the ice broke up in the wintry Missouri River. They had crossed the Rocky Mountains twice and seen the Pacific Ocean. Their journey was nearly at an end.

Since they had split from Lewis and his group of volunteers, Clark had been relying on Charbonneau's Indian wife, Sacagawea, for guidance as they left the land of her ancestors and moved toward the home of her adopted people, the Mandans and Hidatsas. Her advice and guidance had been a boon to the expedition since their meeting in North Dakota. And her small son, Pomp, or Pompey, as he was called by the men, who had joined the expedition during the waning days of winter before the group left the Mandan and had spent his first year in his mother's cradleboard or arms as they crossed the wild expanse of country, was the joy of the expedition.

Clark was especially fond of little Pomp. He enjoyed having him and his mother in his dugout as they crossed the plains. The toddler must have reminded even the young, single, rugged mountain men of the expedition of a life at home and future happiness.

When a giant sandstone block rose up before them as they headed down the Yellowstone River, the explorers must have known that it was a landmark to the local tribes—its sheer size and presence, standing solitary on the prairie, was a signal to all. It was also covered with markings and rock cairns, left for what purpose we can never know for sure.

But whatever the impulse is that causes humans to make their mark on such places, Clark was infected with it, as well. He shouted down from the top of the rock that he could see the mountains rising to the west and the plains rolling to the east. And when he climbed down, he carved his name and the date into the soft rock.

In his journal Clark named the giant rock "Pompey's Tower" for the little boy who traveled with his mother and the explorers across the rolling plains and shining mountains and back again. His signature on the rock is the only remaining physical evidence that the expedition left of its presence.

Clark's affection for Pomp extended beyond his naming of the landmark for the small boy. When the expedition reached the Mandan villages, he offered to adopt the boy and educate him and raise him as a white child in the East. Sacagawea and Charbonneau wouldn't agree to give their son up immediately, but eventually Jean Baptiste did go to Clark for his education, and he became a world traveler before returning to the West as an adult.

# ENCOUNTER WITH THE BLACKFEET

## July 26–27, 1806

Lewis raised his spyglass and looked into the distance. The craggy peaks of the mountains were far to the west now, and the great rolling plains that they had passed over the previous summer stretched as far east as he could see. His small band was content with the sight of bison grazing peacefully on the thick, rich grass. Finally, they had fresh meat after months of dried fish and roots. If only Drouillard would return with the horses that had run away.

Through the glass of his instrument, Lewis spotted something—about thirty horses! But they weren't riderless, as he had hoped. The men on these mounts must be the Blackfeet, or Piegan, Indians that the friendly Nez Perce and Shoshone had told him of. And they were watching Drouillard, alone on horseback in the distance and unaware of their presence.

Ever since Lewis's small crew had split off from the main expedition at the beginning of July, he'd feared an encounter with the fierce Blackfeet. They were the enemies of the Shoshone and Nez Perce and were feared by other plains tribes, as well. The Blackfeet had horses, and they had guns. They were also relatively wealthy from trading with the British fur traders to the north in Canada, and they were mistrustful of whites.

Conquering his fear, Lewis began the slow ride toward the band, which was probably about a mile away. He decided that the friendly approach—as if he'd never heard of the raids made against other tribes or any other word of this band—was probably best. When they finally made contact after a tense game of approach and retreat, Lewis gave them medals and a flag, and they all smoked a pipe together as a sign of friendship.

With things going so well, Lewis made another move. The Piegan should camp with his small band that night while they talked. After they agreed, he told them that he had already made peace with the Shoshone, Nez Perce, and Salish and wanted to do the same with them. He wanted them to stop trading with the British to the north and instead only trade with whites who came from the east. They would offer guns and other goods in trade.

This was bad news for the Piegan. If this white man had made peace with their enemies and was planning to give them guns, their advantage would be gone. The other tribes could band together against them. Whether because of a misunderstanding of translation or a genuine problem with the proposals Lewis had made, things were about to get worse.

During the night each member of the Corps of Discovery took a turn at watch, and all passed peacefully. But at dawn things took a turn. One of the Piegan—one who had been given a medal by Lewis the day before—grabbed a rifle that Joseph Field had laid down and another from under the head of Reubin Field. And at the same moment, two others grabbed Lewis's and Drouillard's guns.

Joseph and Reubin ran after their disappearing weapons and stabbed the Piegan as they retrieved them. Lewis awoke in the scuffle and, when he found his own rifle gone, took aim with his pistol. The frightened Indian dropped Lewis's rifle, and Lewis refused to allow his men to shoot him.

But the Piegan weren't finished with these white men. They next tried to drive off the horses, which would have stranded the group. This was serious. When Lewis took aim again, his bullet shot through the stomach of one of the Indians, and Lewis said he felt a bullet whiz by his head when the wounded man took aim and fired at him.

Within a few minutes the skirmish would be over, and after retrieving the flag they had given the Blackfeet the night before and taking some meat and horses from what remained of the camp, Lewis and his men remounted and fled east. At two in the morning, after riding hard with few breaks for rest and food, they came to a camp near today's Fort Benton, Montana, where they slept, exhausted.

Lewis's skirmish with the Blackfeet is a favorite topic for historians because of the ramifications that the incident had on future relations with the tribe as trappers and settlers moved into Montana. We can't know if a friendship might have been forged with the Blackfeet if the incident hadn't occurred, but it does stand as a black mark on the record of the expedition's usually peaceful encounters with indigenous peoples of the West.

# WOUNDED

## August 11–12, 1806

Meriwether Lewis was in agony when at last the pirogue pulled in sight of Captain Clark's party. The two halves of the Corps of Discovery had been separated for several weeks as they made the journey back across present-day Montana toward home. Their adventures had been many, but perhaps none so perilous as what had Lewis flat on his stomach in the bottom of the boat, ready to hand off his journal to his friend and cocaptain as soon as he was able.

As always, hunting was a main object of the expedition as they made their way cross-country in the canoes and on foot, especially now that they were back in the home of the buffalo, elk, deer, and grizzly. On the morning of August 11, 1806, Lewis had seen a grizzly, which got wind of them and ran off; shot a buffalo that had been swimming in the river and that was unfit to eat when the men went to dress it; and sent another party after a herd of elk.

The thought of fresh meat must have been a strong enticement for action. Almost as soon as he sent one party away after the large elk herd, Lewis saw more of the handsome animals in a willow thicket nearby. He ordered Cruzatte, who was a bit nearsighted, to come with him into the thicket in search of the elk.

The pair had luck almost immediately. They shot two fine elk—killing one and wounding the other—and split up to finish the wounded animal off. All at once, as he moved through the underbrush, Lewis felt a sharp pain as hot lead ripped through his thigh. It missed the bone, he surmised, as he screamed in agony, but it was a painful wound.

"Damn you, you have shot me," he called out to Cruzatte. It must have been his nearsighted hunting companion who mistook him for the wounded elk—all dressed in his leather clothes.

Cruzatte did not answer—no one answered. Lewis became convinced that it had not been Cruzatte, after all. Indians must have crept up on him and fired. Now, he was in great pain and feared for the rest of his party. He must get back to the canoes and report on the situation and get help for his wound.

With difficulty Lewis ran back for the canoes, calling for Cruzatte to retreat and ordering the men to take up their arms. When he arrived back at the canoes, Cruzatte was not there, but he ordered the rest of the men to follow him into the thicket in search of the Indians. After a few steps it was clear that he could not go on, but he sent the men on ahead in search of his assailants.

After about twenty minutes the men returned, with an alarmed Cruzatte in tow. They had seen no Indians, but Cruzatte denied shooting Lewis and claimed he'd never heard his cries, either. Lewis was skeptical that Cruzatte's hearing had joined his eyesight in impairment, but he realized the shooting was an accident. With Sergeant Gass's help, he cleaned his wound as best he could—pulled a ball that matched Cruzatte's short rifle from his thigh—and prepared to go on his way.

When on the next day, Clark's party saw their comrades coming over the rise, Lewis was nowhere in sight. At first Clark was alarmed; what had happened to his good friend over the past weeks? Then, he spotted the leather-clad shape of his cocaptain in the bottom of the canoe, lying on his stomach. After that, the whole story of the expedition's separation must have been told.

Lewis left off writing in his journal as sitting and writing was too painful, leaving his friend to describe the expedition's last days.

# MAYBE HOME IS IN THE ROCKIES

## August 15, 1806

Most of John Colter's companions couldn't believe it when he put the question to them: If he stayed in the wilderness with Joseph Dixon and Forest Hancock, would they all agree to continue on the trip home to St. Louis with the Corps of Discovery? It was a strange question to put to men who'd been far from friends and family, traveling nearly eight thousand miles by canoe, foot, and horse for nearly three years. Most were anxious to find their way back to "civilization" and have a meal that didn't consist of roots, berries, or partially rotted meat. The thought of a good, soft bed must have appealed to some, too.

The number of trappers heading west to the beaver-rich streams of the Rocky Mountains had grown substantially in the years since the forty-member Corps of Discovery launched its keelboat and headed up the Missouri River in hopes of exploring the new Louisiana Purchase and finding a water passage to the West. The price that fashion-conscious city folk would pay for the rich, dark pelts was enough to tempt mountain men with a sense of adventure to pack their own canoes and paddle into the unknown.

On August 11, 1806, the returning expedition had visitors at their camp on the Missouri River. Two dugouts pulled around the bend of the river and Dixon and Hancock stepped out looking for the same thing that Lewis and Clark had been seeking for many months: information about the unknown territory ahead. Even better than information, though, would be the company of one of these hardy explorers who had made their way to and from the Pacific. They could promise anyone who chose to go with them a life of further adventure and the wealth to be had as a fur trapper in the rich lands of the Rocky Mountains. John Colter wanted the job.

Dixon and Hancock returned to the Mandan villages with the expedition, where, on August 15, 1806, John Colter presented his plan to his commanding officers. Lewis and Clark told Colter he might remain behind—get his discharge from the corps early—if the others agreed that they wouldn't ask for similar consideration, and all readily agreed. The men pooled together useful supplies for his return west.

But the expedition did not return to St. Louis a man short. Lewis and Clark convinced one of the Mandan chiefs to go with them to meet President Jefferson in Washington. It was a major coup for an expedition bent on improving relations with the Missouri River Indians.

Colter would spend several more years in the West, traveling and trapping all over the Northern Rockies before returning to St. Louis for good. John Colter lore, including a tale of his miraculous escape from Blackfeet captors and the wild stories he told of a place where water bubbled up out of the ground, is a rich part of the story of the West. For a long time he was credited as being the first white trapper to see the geysers and hot springs in what is now Yellowstone National Park, giving the area the nickname, "Colter's Hell," but most historians now believe that what he saw was actually a hot springs near Cody, Wyoming.

# HUZZAH!

## September 20, 1806

Clark wrote effusively in his journal: "we saw some cows on the bank which was a joyfull Sight to the party and caused a Shout to be raised for joy."

The settlement of La Charrette was in sight, and the men strained at the oars to land on the shore near that friendly village. The traders in boats nearby answered the ringing shots of joy as the men put their feet on the firm American ground and had their first pork, beef, and whiskey for many months. It was September 20, 1806, and the last time the men had seen the village was more than two years past. They were nearly to St. Louis and the start of their journey—they were nearly home!

Every day brought fresh sentiments of joy and greeting from the inhabitants along the shores of the Missouri River. Clark noted that there were more settlements since their departure, and at every turn there were ladies and gentlemen walking out to greet the band of explorers and offering libations and supplies. When the rain started, there were homes to rest in—roofs over their heads that their own muscle and ingenuity did not supply—and they reveled in it.

On Tuesday, September 23, 1806, they reached St. Louis, where they purchased clothes for a Mandan who was accompanying them to Washington, D.C., and wrote letters, and ate, and slept, and relaxed, and rejoiced. They were home at last, and each fine morning they rose and contemplated a day with no pressing need to move a little farther down the river, over the mountains, or across the plains.

The most telling sentiment on the part of their greeters was found at La Charrette. Clark reported: "both French and Americans seem to express great pleasure at our return, and acknowledged themselves much astonished in seeing us return. they informed us that we were supposed to have been long lost since, and were entirely given out by every person &c."

# EPILOGUE

Much of what we know today about the Lewis and Clark Expedition's epic journey to the Pacific Ocean in 1804–1806 comes from the journals kept by the captains and by a few of the other members of the expedition. And, when they were originally edited and published, those journals formed the basis for what people in the United States knew about the Louisiana Territory. Today, our knowledge of the territory (now most of the western United States) has expanded exponentially, but the value of that original report has never been forgotten.

Historians, archaeologists, and those interested in oral tradition have expanded our knowledge of the Lewis and Clark Expedition, but mysteries remain about its members and about the journals themselves. Myth woven with legend woven with fact has made the story of the Corps of Discovery and its personnel one of the most fascinating in American history.

Thomas Jefferson named **Meriwether Lewis** governor of the Louisiana Territory shortly after the expedition's return. He died under mysterious circumstances in an inn located along the Natchez Trace in 1809. He was apparently shot—but whether it was a murder or a suicide remains a matter for debate.

**William Clark** served as governor of the Missouri Territory from 1813 to 1820 and was also in charge of Indian Affairs west of the Mississippi River from 1813 until his death in 1838. Much of what is known about the other members of the expedition came from his notes about their whereabouts written later in his life.

**Jean Baptiste Charbonneau** went to live with Clark in St. Louis when he was six years old and received the education of a privileged American child. When he was eighteen, he went to Europe for six years as the companion of Prince Paul of Wurttemburg, then returned to the West for a career as a mountain man, fur trader, and guide. He died in Oregon in 1866, a man who had seen the opening of the frontier and the end of the Civil War.

**Toussaint Charbonneau** remained an interpreter for various traders and also for Clark and probably died sometime in the 1830s.

**Sacagawea** remains one of the most mysterious members of the Lewis and Clark Expedition. She either died in about 1812, at the age of about twenty-four or twenty-five, near today's Mobridge, South Dakota, or she lived until she was quite an old woman, dying on the Wind River Indian Reservation when she was nearly one hundred years old. Both locations have monuments to this remarkable woman.

**York** was freed by Clark by 1811 and ran a wagon freight company in Tennessee and Kentucky. He died of cholera on his way to meet Clark in St. Louis.

**John Colter,** the man who left the expedition early and went west with trappers, was later given credit for being one of the first white men to describe the wonders of what would become Yellowstone National Park. (Whether or not he actually ever visited the interior of the park is a matter of some debate among historians.)

Most of the enlisted men went on to average lives with families and businesses in the settled parts of the United States, but several went on to some fame as trappers and explorers or served in the War of 1812. All of the veterans of the Lewis and Clark Expedition were given a land grant of 320 acres at its conclusion in addition to their salaries (five dollars a month for the privates) during the period of the expedition. The interpreters received twenty-five dollars a month in pay. Sacagawea and York received nothing.

One of the greatest mysteries of the expedition, however, involves not its participants but the records of the leader, Meriwether Lewis. It was expected by Thomas Jefferson that Lewis would attend to the business of editing and publishing the journals shortly after the return of the expedition, but for reasons not fully understood, no work on the task began until after Lewis's death, when Clark hired Nicholas Biddle to prepare a published edition of the records of the two captains on their journey. (Several of the other members of the expedition did have their own accounts published.) For several periods during the expedition, only the words of Clark survive—and whether Lewis did not make journal entries for those times or whether they have been lost to history is unknown.

# LEWIS AND CLARK EXPEDITION FACTS AND TRIVIA

- Thomas Jefferson gave the Lewis and Clark Expedition the rather lofty name "Corps of Discovery," but the expedition members did not use that name to describe themselves until after they'd been on the trail for a few months. Apparently, once they started their journey, the truth of the description bore out for even the most skeptical.

- Nearly every animal that Lewis or Clark described as being found in eastern Montana is still resident there today, with the notable exception of the grizzly bear, *Ursus arctos horribilis*, which has moved into a limited range in the western part of the state because of decreased habitat due to human encroachment.

- Giant Springs, near Great Falls, Montana, mentioned by Clark in his journal, is one of the largest natural springs in the world.

- Lewis was technically the highest-ranking officer on the expedition, even though he requested that Clark retain the equal rank of captain. Both referred to each other as "captain" throughout the three-year journey, but Clark was technically a lieutenant until he was promoted posthumously by President Bill Clinton in January 2001.

- There were forty-five men with the expedition when they left Camp Wood. By and large, they were army enlisted men from the Ohio River Valley, but there were also French settlers in the group.

- The men who served in the Corps of Discovery came from Connecticut, Kentucky, Maryland, Massachusetts, New Hampshire, North Carolina, Pennsylvania, Tennessee, Virginia, and what is now the state of Missouri.

- When the expedition left the Rocky Mountains heading west in fall 1805, they left official US territory until they crossed into the mountains again in the spring of 1806.

- The expedition knew about the Continental Divide before they crossed it, because it was well known that water flowed west into the Pacific Ocean and east into the Atlantic Ocean. They just didn't know how high or impenetrable the Rocky Mountains would be.

- There was a possibility of at least part of the expedition returning to the United States by ship if they met up with one on the Pacific coast. However, the timing was off, and they made no contact with trading ships while they were encamped at Fort Clatsop.

- The corps took more than ten tons of gear with them, but even so ran out of trade goods to use in their dealings with the Native Americans along the way. They started cutting the brass buttons off of the officers' coats to use in place of the medals they'd given out earlier.

- Each man on the expedition needed to eat about eight pounds of fat meat (their main food) each day to keep up his strength.

- As early as June 8, 1804, the expedition met trappers coming downriver from the west. They extracted as much information from them about what to expect in their journey as they could, but even so much was still unknown.

- Most of the men were sick for part of the journey—probably with dysentery—due to their unvarying diet of meat, some of which was at least partially spoiled. Scientists wouldn't discover for another fifty years that bacteria and germs were responsible for that kind of illness.

- Of the injuries and illnesses on the trip, the only fatality was Sergeant Charles Floyd, who probably died of peritonitis following a ruptured appendix on August 20, 1804. He was only twenty or twenty-one.

- On August 22, 1804, the first election by Americans west of the Mississippi was held. Private Gass was chosen to replace Floyd as sergeant.

- Lewis was eager to fulfill Jefferson's aims for the expedition. He began his collection of unusual plants before they even left Camp Wood, Illinois, in 1804, with a sample of the Osage orange.

- Lewis probably gained much of his knowledge of botany and skill with medicinal plants from his mother, Lucy Meriwether Lewis, who was a skilled herbalist.

- As the expedition crossed the Kansas River, its members identified a flock of green-and-yellow birds that are now thought to be Carolina parakeets. Sadly, the last survivor of this species died in the Cincinnati Zoo in 1918. Among the other birds that they encountered were pelicans, bald eagles, and giant condors.

- Overall, the expedition brought back descriptions of 178 plants and 122 animals encountered on their journey.

- The captains had heard much about the Great White Bear (grizzly) that inhabited the Great Plains and Rocky Mountains. Their first encounter with the animals was a paw print sighting at what is now Bismarck, North Dakota.

- The humble prairie dog was an animal of much interest to the expedition members. They roasted and ate one—and captured one to return it live to Thomas Jefferson.

- Pierre Cruzatte carried his violin with him cross-country and often entertained his comrades in camp.

- The Corps of Discovery carried quite an arsenal with them up the Missouri. They had rifles, muskets, pistols, a small cannon, and two blunderbusses as a part of the official arms of the expedition, and many of the men carried their own civilian weapons, as well.

- Both Lewis and Clark would eventually live in St. Louis as governors of the Louisiana Territory. The site of the great arch now covers the ground that once held their homes.

- A mystery about the existence of the journal kept by Lewis from May 20, 1804, to February 1805 persists to this day. Some historians believe that he had a full account of those months that was lost either before returning to St. Louis or after. Others say that he simply didn't make a detailed record of that part of the expedition.

# BIBLIOGRAPHY

Ambrose, Stephen E. *Undaunted Courage: Meriwether Lewis, Thomas Jefferson, and the Opening of the American West.* New York: Simon & Schuster, 1996.

Betts, Robert B. *In Search of York: The Slave Who Went to the Pacific with Lewis and Clark.* Boulder: Colorado Associated University Presses, 1985.

DeVoto, Bernard, ed. *The Journals of Lewis and Clark.* Boston: Houghton Mifflin, 1953.

Fifer, Barbara and Vicky Soderberg. *Along the Trail with Lewis and Clark.* Helena: Montana Magazine, 1998.

Gold Thwaites, Reuben, ed. *Original Journals of the Lewis and Clark Expedition.* New York: Dodd, Meade, and Company, 1905.

Hunsaker, Joyce Badgley. *Sacagawea Speaks: Beyond the Shining Mountains with Lewis and Clark.* Helena, MT: TwoDot Books, 2000.

MacGregor, Carol Lynn, ed. *The Journals of Patrick Gass, Member of the Lewis and Clark Expedition.* Missoula, MT: Mountain Press Publishing, 1997.

Moulton, Gary E., ed. *The Journals of the Lewis & Clark Expedition.* 10 vols. Lincoln: University of Nebraska Press, 1983.

Ronda, James P. *Lewis and Clark among the Indians.* Lincoln: University of Nebraska Press, 1985.

———. *Voyages of Discovery.* Helena: Montana Historical Society Press, 1998.

# BIBLIOGRAPHY

Schmidt, Thomas. *National Geographic's Guide to the Lewis and Clark Trail*. Washington, DC: The National Geographic Society, 1998.

Schullery, Paul. *Lewis and Clark among the Grizzlies*. Helena, MT: Falcon Publishing, 2002.

# INDEX

# ABOUT THE AUTHOR

Erin H. Turner has a degree in history and gender and women's studies from Grinnell College and has lived most of her life in the West along the trails of the pioneers and great explorers. She currently lives in Helena, Montana, near "The Gates of the Mountains" with her husband, Ross Johnson, and their two daughters. She is a full-time writer and editor.